GOT HOPE?

A Devotional Journey through 1 Peter

STANLEY D. GALE

GOT HOPE?

A Devotional Journey through 1 Peter

Got Hope?
A Devotional Journey through 1 Peter

Stanley D. Gale

Copyright © 2024 Stanley D. Gale

ISBN: 979-8-9906725-0-5

Cover design and typeset by www.greatwriting.org

Printed in the United States of America

Waxed Tablet Publications is the imprint for The Fellowship of Ailbe. A waxed tablet was a flat, hand-sized piece of wood covered with beeswax. Notes could be etched in the wax, which could be reused after smoothing. It was used by Medieval monks for note-taking as they journeyed.

For Nathan and Kate and their firstborn, Juniper Joy

"The LORD bless you out of Zion,
and may you see the good of Jerusalem
all the days of your life.
Yes, may you see your children's children."
(Psalm 128:5–6)

Contents

Acknowledgments

I am grateful to Jim Holmes of Great Writing for his input and expertise in bringing this book to life. I am appreciative of T. M. Moore for his faithful service to Christ's kingdom and his friendship and encouragement to me in my ministry. The writing of this book has reminded me of the wonderful theological training I received at Westminster Theological Seminary and the relationships that have endured over the years.

To the Reader

Imagine you are visiting your physician, and hear the familiar words, "The Doctor will see you now." You walk into his office. A voice says, "And how are you today?" and after a moment's surprise you realize that you are in the presence of the apostle Peter! The result of his brief spiritual consultation is that he wants one of his skilled staff—a doctor he has trained—to see you briefly on a daily basis over the next couple of months. What a privilege!

We experience something like that in these pages. First Peter is medicine for our times. It is the prescription we need to live for Christ in the early twenty-first century. And Peter's clinical assistant, Dr. Stanley Gale, is ideally equipped to help us grow to healthy spiritual maturity. He knows how to interpret and apply Peter's principles, and he has extensive experience as a pastor and physician of the soul. His *Got Hope?* can therefore safely be prescribed for every age and stage in the Christian life. So, take the prescription regularly and finish the course of treatment; it will do you good!

SINCLAIR B. FERGUSON
Chancellor's Professor of Systematic Theology, Reformed Theological Seminary
Teaching Fellow, Ligonier Ministries

"Blessed be the God and Father of our Lord Jesus Christ,
who according to His abundant mercy
has begotten us again to a living hope
through the resurrection of Jesus Christ from the dead."
(1 Peter 1:3–4)

Introduction

LIVING HOPE

What is the relationship between hope and home? It is that connection that the apostle Peter explains in his first epistle and it makes all the difference for us as Christians as we navigate the challenging terrain of life in this fallen world en route to glory.

Peter addresses his letter to pilgrims (1 Peter 1:1). Pilgrims are travelers in a land that is not their home, not as vacationers but as sojourners. Paradoxically, we were once at home in this world but now we are like fish out of water, strangers in a familiar land (Heb. 11:13). Our Lord Jesus describes us as being *in* the world (John 17:11) but not *of* it (John 17:14).

So when Peter writes to pilgrims, we want to lean in to hear what he has to say because we are cut from the same cloth and carry the same call as the first recipients of his letter. Peter helps us to understand who we are, what we wrestle with, and how we are to conduct ourselves as ones who bear the name of Jesus.

As pilgrims we are not meanderers, biding our time and leisurely wandering. Rather, we are on mission—kingdom mission. Like the Old Testament figure Daniel was an influence for the living and true God in a land that was not his own, so we are to be influencers for Christ in this world. By our words and deeds, we are to let our light so shine that others might take note and give glory to our Father in heaven. Peter writes to explain how we go about that.

Peter speaks in terms of giving a defense for the hope that is in us (1 Peter 3:15). Often we think of hope as merely a yearning or as an expression of wishful thinking. We hope it doesn't rain, or we hope our car doesn't break down. But the hope Peter speaks of is quite different. The Bible's hope is a confident expectation, a vibrant certainty, an assured conviction. It is sure and steadfast, something definite not iffy.

The reason why the Bible's hope is unshakeable is that it rests on the purpose of an unchanging God and the finished work of Jesus Christ. When Paul writes about hope to the church at Thessalonica, he says of us as Christians that we do not grieve as do the rest who have no hope (1 Thess. 4:13). Those whose home is this world are described as without God and without hope in this world (Eph. 2:12). That hope differentiates us as believers from non-believers and distinguishes us as belonging to God.

What exactly is the surety of our hope? Paul explains, "For God did not appoint us to wrath, but to obtain salvation through our Lord Jesus Christ" (1 Thess. 5:9). The writer of Hebrews paints this picture for us: "We might have strong consolation, who have fled for refuge to lay hold of the hope set before us. This hope we have as an anchor of the soul, both sure and steadfast, and which enters the Presence behind the veil, where the forerunner has entered for us, even Jesus, having become High Priest forever" (Heb. 6:18–20).

Just as Paul and the writer of Hebrews exalt Christ as the basis of our hope, so does Peter: "Blessed be the God and Father of our Lord Jesus Christ, who according to His abundant mercy has begotten us again to a living hope through the resurrection of Jesus Christ from the dead" (1 Peter 1:3). Our hope has life because Jesus lives in resurrection victory and power for us. Peter will keep this hope before us as we press on as travelers. It's so easy to lose our bearings, to grow weary and lose heart. But Peter lifts our eyes to Jesus. He is with us to the very end of the age, that is, through the entirety of our pilgrimage in this world until He takes us to the place He has prepared for us in glory.

Here we see the connection between hope and home. Immediately after writing of the wonder of God's saving work in our lives through the hope of the gospel, Peter highlights the heavenly home that awaits us at the close of our earthly sojourning and that fills us now with eager anticipation. He describes our home as "an inheritance incorruptible and undefiled and that does not fade away, reserved in heaven for you, who are kept by the power of God through faith for salvation ready to be revealed in the last time" (1 Peter 1:4–5). Do you see the certainty? Our inheritance is kept intact for us and we are kept in place for it.

This description echoes the words of Jesus that Peter heard in the upper room on the eve of Christ's betrayal, arrest, and crucifixion. "And if I go and prepare a place for you, I will come again and receive you to Myself; that where I am, there you may be also" (John 14:3). Being with Jesus! No wonder Peter will stress that our struggles now are infused with joy (1 Peter 1:6) in the certainty of seeing our Savior (1 Peter 1:8).

Ours is a living hope, bound up in the living Lord. Moreover, it is a hope for living. Just as we live by faith, so we live from hope. Throughout his epistle, Peter will explain how this hope works itself out in obedience, confidence, courage, and eagerness to honor the Lord Jesus. It affects us in our relationship with God, with fellow believers, with the world around us, and reaches to our inner being.

The devotions of this small book develop Peter's first letter in bite-size pieces. They function as rations for the journey, leading us to partake of the sustenance of God's Word for our spiritual nourishment and growth in grace. Like foods that pair well together, we will see how Peter builds and blends one portion with another that not only provide us nourishment but also stimulate our spiritual senses to taste and see that the Lord is good. Prayer can act as the digestive juices of faith that help us assimilate that truth to strengthen us for the journey.

Each meditation contains a heading that captures the gist of the reading, a portion of the particular text from 1 Peter within view, observations and applications from that passage, and a principle for reflection and application. The devotional format is intended to both inform and inspire. The content of each portion can be partaken in individual communion with God or, by its brevity, can be read and reflected upon with others without prior preparation.

We all know what it's like to be away from home. Home reflects safety, security, and stability. Home is a welcome thought during even the most exhilarating of vacations. How much more welcome is home when, like those who have headed off to war, we return from the adversity, upheaval, and constant danger of the battlefield to the embrace of love, the familiarity of family, and surroundings of peace? Such is the tone of Peter's letter when he alerts us to temporal danger and hardship now but eternal glory to come for all who are known by Jesus Christ. Because He lives, our hope is alive and is to be lived out each passing day.

Chapter 1

Peter the Pastor

"Peter, an apostle of Jesus Christ. . ."
(1 Peter 1:1)

Pastors are shepherds. One of the jobs of a shepherd is to walk with his sheep, particularly in those difficult times of life, times when they feel alone or helpless or scared.

The pastor's personal presence is a great tool for ministry. To sit by someone about to undergo surgery and pray with him, helping him cast his anxieties on God, carries great meaning. Rushing to the side of a couple who have just received devastating news about their child and enfolding them in embrace communicates something mere words could not.

But a pastor brings more than his personal presence. He brings Jesus. He is glad for the warm welcome extended to him when he shows up in times of distress. He knows, though, that he eventually wants to direct their attention to Him who is able to do immeasurably more than all they can ask or imagine. Amidst their anguish, he wants to lift their eyes to Jesus.

In the final chapter of his first letter, Peter will include himself among those who shepherd the flock, calling himself a "fellow elder" (5:1). That is not, however, how he introduces himself in his salutation. There, after giving his name, he says he is "an apostle of Jesus Christ."

Not only does that mean he was included among the twelve our Lord chose to walk with Him in His earthly ministry, being an apostle speaks to the authority of our Lord Jesus Himself. Peter is an elder, engaging himself in the shared ministry to the flock that is Christ's church, but he also holds a position that no pastor today holds. As an apostle, Peter writes with the authority of the Holy Spirit (2 Peter 1:20–21). His letters are included in the canon of Holy Scripture and are to be received as the Word of God they are.

It is on the note of authority that Peter begins his letter. He is bringing to us the very Word of God. He speaks for Jesus to His sheep. In writing his letter, Peter communicates with apostolic authority and reflects a pastoral heart to those who are hurting.

Those Peter is writing to are scattered and suffering. Peter could not rush to their side to be with them, but he could put pen to paper to convey the comfort of Christ, who most certainly was with them. He could speak the Word of God into their lives to help them find their way and open their eyes to the bigger picture of redemptive reality that enveloped them.

So we pick up Peter's letter and we regard it as the Word of God that it is. Ultimately, we hear the pastoral heart of the Chief Shepherd for His sheep in our distress, confusion, and fear.

PRINCIPLE

Jesus said that His sheep hear His voice.
In what way does He speak to us through Peter?

Chapter 2

Foreknowledge of the Father

". . .elect according to the foreknowledge of God the Father. . ."
(1 Peter 1:2)

Many public places will have a lost-and-found bin, a collection point for items discarded or disregarded. Someone will lose her sunglasses and go to the front desk where she will be directed to a motley collection of things found. She will make her way to the bin and begin to rummage through strata of articles lost over weeks and months. She spots her sunglasses but upon closer look realizes hers are a slightly different style. So she digs deeper.

As pilgrims in this world, we can seem like those lost items among a population of lost items, resembling others that make up the human race. While Peter's letter is considered a general epistle in that it is not written to a specific local church, such as the church in Rome, it is not general in that it is written to the entire populace. Rather, Peter writes to a particular people, a peculiar people who stand out as ones claimed by God, as he will later say: "His own special people" (2:9).

Peter describes us as "elect." We are pilgrims in this world as the elect of God. We have been chosen by the Father. He set His love on us from before the foundation of the world and sent His Son to redeem us for His own possession. We are sealed with the Holy Spirit, a seal of ownership to God and inclusion in His family along with others.

It might seem that we are indistinguishable from others in the mass of humanity around us. But God knows those who are His. He will not lose us. He will not lose track of us. He will never discard us or disregard us. We are safe in His arms.

Our status as elect relates to the foreknowledge of God. That says a lot more than we might think. God did not look down the halls of human history to see those who would turn to Him and then set a seal of ownership upon them to make sure they would all be accounted for in the last day. That puts the cart before the theological horse. God did not foresee us; He foreknew us. There is a difference. God foreknew us by setting His love on us before the foundation of the world. He took us as His very own not because of anything attractive or worthy about us but solely because of His divine purpose.

So when Peter writes to "pilgrims . . . elect according to the foreknowledge of God the Father" (1:1), he is addressing us as the objects of God's redeeming love. He is speaking to us amidst the mass of humanity to remind us that we are not alone, not abandoned. Our God is for us and with us, and even now through His Word is speaking to minister to us in the struggles of our pilgrimage.

To the sojourner unsettled in this world and undergoing distress and even persecution, those words are balm to the soul and ballast in the storm. We are known by God. He is our Father. The love He set upon us for His own glory will not waver or weaken, but will hold us fast.

PRINCIPLE

Throughout your days, you belong to your Father in heaven.
What comfort can you gain from that truth?

Chapter 3

Sanctification of the Spirit

". . .in sanctification of the Spirit. . ."
(1 Peter 1:2)

We can endure suffering much better when we know there is purpose behind it. For example, I will actually schedule an appointment with my dentist knowing full well that pain, assault, and mouthal manhandling await me in dealing with a cavity discovered on the previous routine checkup. I endure that suffering because I know that it is the road to resolution of a problem.

Peter is writing to those undergoing all sorts of suffering. He assures them and us that the hardships of our lives are not arbitrary but meaningful. They carry the purpose of God. My dental procedure carried the purpose of the clinician to make me whole. He had discovered decay that needed to be excised and replaced with a filling that would allow me to chew properly and avoid greater problems were it left unattended. In similar fashion, our all-wise God works through the trials of our lives for our holiness.

Holiness lies at the heart of sanctification. Holiness is akin to wholeness in that the image of God disfigured by the fall is restored in knowledge, righteousness, and holiness. In Christ, we are holy and called to be holy. As theologians might put it, our sanctification is definitive in that we stand holy in Christ (1 Cor. 1:30) and it is developmental in that we grow in holiness (1 Cor. 1:2). We are distinct from the world that walks to the beat of its own drum and we are called by God to live in a manner that reflects that distinction of belonging to Him.

Our holiness, however, is not a self-help project, not mere reformation shaped by our self-appointed resolutions. It is the work of the Holy Spirit. It is He who unites us to Christ, He who brings us from spiritual death to spiritual life, He who enables us to die more and more to sin and live increasingly to righteousness. The Spirit is the One who forms Christ in us.

We are God's workmanship, and the suffering we experience contributes to His craftsmanship. The Spirit empowers us and gives us the grace and wisdom necessary for the conduct of our lives in keeping with the Word of God. The efforts we make show results by God's handiwork.

Peter reminds us that whatever adversity we are experiencing, whatever hardship we are enduring, whatever suffering we undergo, God has not lost sight of the plot. It's all part of His plan, just as it was for His Son in His mission as Messiah.

In his sermon to the throngs gathered for Pentecost, Peter framed the suffering of Jesus in terms of being delivered to death "by the determined purpose and foreknowledge of God" (Acts 2:23). The suffering of our lives also carries the determined purpose and foreknowledge of God for us to the accomplishment of His goals—in this case, our sanctification, carried out by the Spirit who indwells us.

PRINCIPLE

In Christ we are holy and called to be holy.
What does it mean to be holy?

Chapter 4

Obedience and Sprinkling
of the Blood

". . .for obedience and sprinkling of the blood of Jesus Christ. . ."
(1 Peter 1:2)

When our house is on fire, there's no sense cleaning the kitchen. That's one extreme. The other is to wonder why we should make our bed when we are just going to sleep in it again. These extremes each contain a common theme, which is that there are situations that absolve us of guilt or relieve us of our responsibilities.

That can be our thinking when we are being persecuted for our faith or find ourselves in the deep end of suffering. Surely, we can let things slide a bit given the circumstances. We certainly don't want to call attention to ourselves and become subject to scrutiny and greater suffering. Do we?

The Old Testament figure Daniel models the answer. Daniel had been among the captives taken from Israel and settled in the foreign land of Babylon. His intention was not to call attention to himself, but that attention was inevitable as he distinguished himself by walking with and serving a God contrary to the gods of the Babylonians. Daniel became known for his allegiance to the Lord. He found himself in a circumstance of suffering as an exile and he opened himself to greater suffering by his overt fidelity to the living God and his refusal to compromise.

Peter is writing to believers in similar circumstances, many of them scattered and suffering, undergoing persecution for their faith. Yet in his salutation, even before he gets to the body of his letter, Peter urges his readers to obedience. Chosen "for obedience" (1 Peter 1:2), he says.

That's because his readers were Christians, those set apart by

God and sanctified by the Spirit. They were sojourners, citizens of another kingdom, heirs of a heavenly home. If they had received Christ as Lord, they were to follow Christ as Lord, in private and in public.

Throughout his letter, Peter will address this no-excuses, no-exceptions approach to life for us as believers in a world that is no friend of Christ. Obedience is one of the ways we glorify God and distinguish ourselves as belonging to Him. It is a means by which we demonstrate the lordship of Christ to an unbelieving world and provoke their demand for an explanation of why we live as we do.

We are the redeemed of the Lord. We are cleansed by the blood of Jesus Christ, who loved us and gave His life for us. Our obedience does not earn us any favor with God. It is by Christ's obedience and shed blood that we are saved, which Peter will later remind us: "who Himself bore our sins in His own body on the tree, that we, having died to sins, might live for righteousness" (1 Peter 2:24). Yet, as sojourners, we are to live lives consecrated to our God and conspicuous of His grace (see Titus 2:11–14).

PRINCIPLE

Obedience means conformity to the will of the God we love.
How is obedience a symptom of our salvation?

Chapter 5

Grace and Peace

"Grace to you and peace be multiplied."
(1 Peter 1:2)

"Good morning!" is a typical way to greet one another when we rise to face another day. It conveys attentive warmth. Underlying the expression is more of a sentiment than a declaration, more "I wish you a good morning" than "It is a good morning."

Ordinarily, we don't give much thought to such casual greetings. They are just a way of welcome, ice breakers to an encounter. Such can be the case when we read the epistles of the New Testament. Grace and peace are common greetings in the epistles of Paul. Peter extends them in both his letters. They are so familiar we can be tempted to gloss over them. Yet this tandem, grace and peace, are rich in meaning to believers. They belong to the DNA of our salvation and set the tone for our relationship with God and one another.

Grace speaks to the underserved, unexpected, unmerited favor of God. It is the sole reason we stand as we do in a reconciled relationship with Him. It points us to what has been bestowed upon us as a gift. We are debtors to grace. While mercy spares us the penalty of sin we deserve, grace lavishes upon us the riches of salvation we do not deserve. Like a condemned prisoner on death row, we languish as the day of our execution draws near, with no ground or expectation of reprieve. There is absolutely nothing we can do to make up for sins past or to measure up to righteousness required. Against the backdrop of our guilt, God speaks to us grace.

Coupled with grace is peace. If grace is the outpouring, then peace is the outcome. Because of God's grace, we who were at enmity with Him, alienated from Him in our sin, enjoy peace with God through His reconciling work in Christ on our behalf. We have peace with God and know the peace of God. Peter speaks to us as ones who possess a redemptive and resounding peace, even in the midst of our suffering as sojourners.

Just as "Good morning" can be understood as shorthand for "I wish you a good morning," so "grace and peace" can be seen as shorthand for bestowal of blessing. In a sense Peter is opening on a note of benediction pronounced over the years by the old covenant priesthood: "The LORD bless you and keep you; the LORD make His face shine upon you, and be gracious to you; the LORD lift up His countenance upon you, and give you peace" (Num. 6:24–26). That grace and peace is lavished upon us through Christ, which Peter spells out in his second letter: "Grace and peace be multiplied to you in the knowledge of God and of Jesus our Lord" (2 Peter 1:2; cf. 1 Peter 5:14).

Peter not only extends grace and peace to us in Christ; he expresses that it be multiplied. He wants us to grow in the grace and knowledge of our Lord Jesus. Situations of adversity do not stifle grace and peace for us. Rather, they open the nozzle wide for us to know more fully what is ours in Christ.

PRINCIPLE

Grace and peace are not mere sentiments.
In what way are they core values to our standing before God?

Chapter 6

Blessed be the God and Father

"Blessed be the God and Father of our Lord Jesus Christ. . ."
(1 Peter 1:3)

Imagine you are destitute, have no money to buy food, and have not eaten for some time. What would your reaction be to someone who took notice of you and spread before you a feast? Your heart would be filled with gratitude, and you would likely be prompted to bless the person. As does Paul in opening the body of his letter to the Ephesians (Eph. 1:3), so Peter begins on the high note of blessing Him from whom all blessings flow. Blessing is the reflex of the beneficiary.

Blessing God is an expression of worship. We ascribe to God the glory due His name. We bless Him for who He is as Creator, and for what He has done as Redeemer. Like taking as deep a breath as possible to exert the loudest and longest note of praise, the psalmist reaches to the depths of his being: "Bless the Lord, O my soul; and all that is within me, bless His holy name!" (Ps. 103:1). Although David would later in the psalm describe the character of God to provoke praise, he begins by speaking of what God had done as Redeemer. "Bless the Lord, O my soul, and forget not all His benefits" (Ps. 103:2). He goes on to inventory those benefits.

In the same way, Peter rouses us to bless God for what He has done. Not surprisingly, since he is writing to pilgrims, Peter celebrates God's wondrous mercy in giving us a home in heaven. Before he details that heavenly hope, however, Peter focuses our attention on God. It is easy for us to lose sight of God when we are beset by troubles. Peter learned this lesson personally. When he was in a boat rocked by a storm-tossed sea and he saw Jesus walking toward him on the water, he asked Jesus to allow him to walk on the water to Him (Matt. 14:22–33). At his Lord's bidding, Peter stepped out of the boat but when he took his eyes off Jesus and turned his attention to the tumultuous sea, he began to sink. Jesus graciously responded to Peter's cry for help. We can take our eyes off Jesus, both in adversity and in abundance.

Now writing to people who are engulfed in the storm of suffering, Peter directs their eyes and ours to God. Peter identifies Him as "the God and Father of our Lord Jesus Christ." Peter particularly wants us to see God in His eternal, transcendent glory. He directs our attention to God who has sent His Son for us and our salvation. Peter may well have had in mind the voice of God the Father from the cloud on the Mount of Transfiguration: "This is My beloved Son, in whom I am well pleased. Hear Him!" (Matt. 17:5; see 2 Peter 1:16–18). Look at Jesus. Listen to Him.

The starting point for navigating the trials of our lives is taking hold of the hand of our God and Father. From that we know certainty, find solace, and gain strength.

PRINCIPLE

Bearings in suffering begin with focus on our God and Father. What does it mean for us to bless God?

Chapter 7

A Living Hope

". . .according to His abundant mercy has begotten us again
to a living hope. . ."
(1 Peter 1:3)

Electric cars have been in the news quite a bit lately, particularly with gas prices going through the roof. One area of concern, however, has been how far EVs can travel on a single charge. Even the most capable of batteries holds the potential of leaving a driver stranded when its charge is depleted.

As Christians, we do not need to be worried about the power needed to reach our destination. Peter tells us we are powered now by the resurrection life of Jesus Christ. Ours is a living hope.

What is a living hope? First, let's understand what hope is. Hope is not wishful thinking. "I hope it doesn't rain." "I hope my team makes the playoffs." That sort of hope is more hope-so. It carries no assurance, only possibility at worst and probability at best. It offers no certainty.

The hope Peter has in mind is something completely different. It carries absolute certainty. Ours is not a hope-so hope but a know-so hope. It engenders confident expectation, assured conviction, and vibrant certainty. It will neither fail nor will it disappoint.

From our experience, even the surest of things can fail. How can Peter speak with such certainty? It's because our hope as Christians is living. The battery will never die. The promise will never fail. Such hope cannot be dashed. It is alive with the resurrection power of Jesus Christ. Our hope lives because Christ lives. Our hope cannot fail because Christ cannot die. He lives and reigns in victory. The writer of Hebrews describes our hope in objective terms in reference to the finished work of Christ. "This hope we have as an anchor of the soul, both sure and steadfast, and which enters the

Presence behind the veil, where the forerunner has entered for us, even Jesus" (Heb. 6:19–20).

The hope that is ours in Christ gives us encouragement, comfort, and courage. When Paul talks about this hope that belongs to us as believers (1 Thess. 4:13–5:8), he lifts our eyes to what God, in His great mercy, has done for us. "For God did not appoint us to wrath, but to obtain salvation through our Lord Jesus Christ, who died for us, that whether we wake or sleep, we should live together with Him" (1 Thess. 5:9–10).

The reality of our living hope is the peg that Peter drives into the ground, an anchor to our soul in the turbulence of a tumultuous world, to give us unshakeable confidence in the handiwork of our God. Just think! Our new birth brings us to participate now in the new life of the age to come, a life abundant, eternal, and uninterrupted. We live in hope because our Hope lives.

PRINCIPLE

Our hope is alive with the life of the risen Christ.
What encouragement and courage do we find in that for our
journey in this world?

Chapter 8

Inheritance

*"...an inheritance incorruptible and undefiled
and that does not fade away..."*
(1 Peter 1:4)

I got caught in traffic behind a large vehicle. It made for a tedious drive with the obstructed view and the slow progress. I did find some amusement, however, when I spotted the bumper sticker attached to the mobile home. "We're spending our children's inheritance." Their children might not have been as amused.

That's the problem with inheritances. We can never be absolutely certain what they will look like when it's time to take possession. The house bequeathed to us may be broken down. Promised finances may be depleted. Plus, what happens if we die before our parents and are not around to receive the inheritance, or because we somehow displeased our parents, we are disinherited?

Peter speaks to us as pilgrims on a journey, away from home, and tells us of a radically different inheritance. It's like a family living in squalor receiving a letter from a law firm telling them they are heirs of a vast estate. That news brings them comfort and joy, anticipation and longing. It assures them that their suffering and sojourning are of limited duration. It infuses in them strength for today and bright hope for tomorrow.

In Christ, as ones enfolded into the family of God, we are heirs. An inheritance awaits us. The question is, though, what will that inheritance look like when we take hold of it, that is, if we take possession of it? Will we be disappointed? Should we temper our excitement?

Peter allays such fears by describing our inheritance as "incorruptible and undefiled and that does not fade away, reserved in heaven for you" (1 Peter 1:4). In other words, what is laid up for us in our heavenly home now will be ours in pristine, undepleted, spectacular fullness later. Our name is already on the door and has been prepared for us.

But what if something happens to us? Can we be disinherited by our disobedience and rebellion? Peter says God has got that aspect covered as well. We have been born again into the family of God and we are "kept by the power of God through faith for salvation ready to be revealed in the last time" (1 Peter 1:5). Peter holds up the promise of Christ: "This is the will of the Father who sent Me, that of all He has given Me I should lose nothing, but should raise it up at the last day. And this is the will of Him who sent Me, that everyone who sees the Son and believes in Him may have everlasting life; and I will raise him up at the last day" (John 6:39–40).

Peter lets us know that God has both bases covered. Our inheritance is kept for us, and we are kept for our inheritance. That means that when we find ourselves shaken and insecure now, we can turn our thoughts to know that nothing in all creation will be able to separate us from the love of God for us in Christ Jesus.

PRINCIPLE

Our hope is in Christ and our home is with Christ.
In what way is our heavenly home the same as our heavenly hope?

Chapter 9

Reason for Rejoicing

"In this you greatly rejoice. . ."
(1 Peter 1:6)

What do you say to cheer someone up when he or she is going through tough times? "Hang in there, it couldn't get any worse." "It only hurts when you breathe." "I know it's unbearable but somebody out there has it worse than you do, probably." Silliness aside, even well-intentioned, sincere, thoughtful efforts can fall short or ring hollow in the face of overwhelming distress.

Peter, however, brings to bear the ultimate encouragement. He begins by saying, "In this you greatly rejoice" (v. 6) and goes on to speak of rejoicing with "joy inexpressible and full of glory" (v. 8). Such is the intensity of this joy that it dispels the darkness of despair and washes out any lesser light of encouragement.

What is the "this" Peter refers to that triggers our joy? It is our inheritance in heaven. We may be weighed down with the adversity of the sojourner now but that is only temporary. Suffering is not the final word. We may be homeless now but we have a permanent abode in heavenly glory. The inheritance of the firstborn is ours through Christ. It is kept for us and we for it. One day!

Peter describes our trial-bearing struggles as being "for a little while" (1:6). It certainly doesn't seem like a little while when we find ourselves in the thick of the trial, weighed down and reeling. On the contrary, it seems interminable, as if it will never end. But it will. The darkness will be swallowed up in glory.

Peter wants us to stand back and look at the bigger picture. He takes us to the vista of eternity. Like one of those maps in the mall, he points out our destination in the new creation and then points to the little "x" on the road to glory and says to us, "You are here." The vastness and wonder of what is in store for us overwhelms our perspective and overshadows our pain. It is on the note of our hope in Christ that Peter will close his letter: "But may the God of all grace, who called us to His eternal glory by Christ Jesus, after you have suffered a while, perfect, establish, strengthen, and settle you" (1 Peter 5:10).

It is this inheritance with all it entails that prompts us to rejoice, a joy that tempers our trials and whets our appetites, a joy that occupies our attention and overrules our sorrows in the present moment. Peter is simply enfolding us into what the Lord Jesus spoke to His disciples in the Upper Room: "These things I have spoken to you, that My joy may remain in you, and that your joy may be full" (John 15:11). Among those things spoken was the assurance of our inheritance (John 14:1–3), that where our Lord is we may be also. By His grace, our Lord Jesus will welcome us, worn and weary from our travail: "Well done, good and faithful servant" (Matt. 25:23).

PRINCIPLE

Our greatest joy is Christ Himself.
How, in adversity, can we rejoice in the Lord?

Chapter 10

Genuineness of Faith

"...the genuineness of your faith..."
(1 Peter 1:7)

I remember watching westerns when I was growing up. One of those memories involved a potential buyer biting down onto a gold piece to test its authenticity. I suppose since pure gold is a soft metal, the bite would leave an impression. The difficulties we face can serve that purpose in our lives. God designs the trials of our lives to test the mettle of our faith.

Peter speaks of our being "grieved by various trials" (1:6). This grief is a companion with joy in our earthly pilgrimage. The struggles and adversity we face cause us to suffer but we are comforted knowing that those trials are temporary, and that we will one day enter the glory our Lord Jesus has prepared for us. Joy and sorrow may seem like strange bedfellows but they will share the space as long as we are in this world, much as was the case with our Lord Jesus, "who for the joy that was set before Him endured the cross" (Heb. 12:2).

Peter explains God's purpose in the grief of our trials: "that the genuineness of your faith, being much more precious than gold that perishes, though it is tested by fire, may be found to praise, honor, and glory at the revelation of Jesus Christ" (1 Peter 1:7). In his Gospel account, Peter's disciple, John Mark, recorded a parable taught by our Lord Jesus in which four soils are described (Mark 4:3–20). The gospel is the seed scattered on the soils. Though Jesus speaks of four soils—hard, rocky, thorny, good—for all intents and purposes there are only two, fruitful soil and unfruitful soil. The seed reacts to the good soil by bearing fruit, testifying to the sovereign grace of God to change the soil of the heart. Two of the soils receive the seed of the gospel and, while there seems to be life because growth does appear, no fruit is produced, thus betraying the lack of good soil.

Faith is a fruit of the implanted Word of God in hearts made receptive and fertile by His Spirit. Trials act to authenticate that faith as a product of the grace of God. Peter is writing to those who are being persecuted and afflicted. Will their faith bear up under the duress of trials? Jesus described this in His soils parable: "And they have no root in themselves, but endure for a while; then, when tribulation or persecution arises on account of the word, immediately they fall away" (Mark 4:17, ESV). This relates to the genuineness of which Peter speaks (1 Peter 1:7).

When we encounter trials of various kinds, intensities, and durations, we want to trace them from the hand that extends them to us to the face of our Father who loves us. We want to embrace the trial, casting our cares upon Him in faith that He cares for us. That eye contact, expectation, and longing attest to His handiwork of grace in our lives.

The genuineness of our faith does not speak to our effort, tenacity, or zeal. Rather, it points us to our loving Father and the grandeur of His amazing grace. The "praise, honor, and glory" (v. 7) of which Peter speaks belong not to us who believe but to Him to whom we belong.

PRINCIPLE

True faith reflects God's handiwork of grace.
In what way is faith a fruit of God's work in our hearts?

Chapter 11

The Joy of Jesus

". . .Jesus Christ, whom having not seen you love."
(1 Peter 1:7–8)

The most wonderful aspect of the inheritance laid up for us will not be property, possessions, safety, or stability. It will be Jesus. Gathered around the table in the upper room with the other disciples, Peter would have been stirred at the words of his Lord: "In My Father's house are many mansions; if it were not so, I would have told you. I go to prepare a place for you. And if I go and prepare a place for you, I will come again and receive you to Myself; that where I am, there you may be also" (John 14:2–3).

Jesus had just informed His disciples that He was going where they could not follow then but would later. Peter was disturbed by the words of his Lord. But Jesus would go on to say, "Let not your heart be troubled" (John 14:1), and proceed to call His disciples to faith and assure them with the promise that they would be with Him.

That is the allure of the Christian's inheritance—being with Jesus. When we hear of a mansion, our minds may go to a sprawling, opulent estate, perhaps gated with a private access road where we are lord of the manor. But the picture Jesus paints could not be more different. What is translated "mansion" simply means a place to dwell. It is translated "home" later in the chapter: "If anyone loves Me, he will keep My word; and My Father will love him, and We will come to him and make Our home with him" (John 14:23).

It's been said home is where the heart is. That is certainly true in the case of our inheritance in glory, because our heart is with Jesus. We long for Him. We long to be with Him in the place He has prepared for us.

How would you define eternal life? Often, we think of it in terms like we would think of a mansion, a gift of monumental proportion, a blessing of salvation that stands in stark contrast to the fires of hell. But no acquisition—no state of being—would be anything without Jesus. Here's how our Lord Himself explained eternal life in the climactic prayer before leaving the upper room with Peter to head out to continue praying in the Garden of Gethsemane: "And this is eternal life, that they may know You, the only true God, and Jesus Christ whom You have sent" (John 17:3).

Peter extends to those who are sojourners, suffering in this world, the promise of home, a home with Jesus, "whom having not seen you love" (v. 8). We rejoice with joy inexpressible and filled with glory at the thought of forever being in communion with Him who loved us and gave Himself for us, who bought us at the price of His own blood.

For now, it's like carrying photographs of ones we love while we are away from them, longing to be at home with them. Though we do not see Jesus now, one day our faith will be sight and we will see Him face to face.

PRINCIPLE

The gain of salvation would be hollow without the gain of our Savior.
How does knowing God relate to eternal life?

Chapter 12

Prophets and Angels

". . .things which angels desire to look into."
(1 Peter 1:12)

W hen we're walking down the street and come upon a crowd gathered, we try to see what's going on, particularly if everyone is looking in the same direction. That's just where Peter brings us, to a horde from history comprised of God's prophets and angels. Prophets were God's spokesmen who brought His word to His people, pointing them toward a future day. Angels are heavenly beings who serve God as heralds, messengers, and executors of His decree. Since the Garden of Eden, God's purposes have been afoot, and both earth and heaven have been on edge to see the fulfillment of His salvation.

At the fall of mankind through the sin of Adam in Genesis 3, God uttered a completely uncalled-for promise. He spoke of the seed of a woman who would do battle and gain victory over the ruler of this present age. With the disobedience of the first man, God could have brought down the curtain on human history, but in keeping with His purpose in redemption, God allowed history to continue. That history would serve as the womb for His promise of a deliverer.

Through the years, God would give more and more detail about this Savior. His person and work would be conveyed through predictions, types, proclamation, and preview. God raised up prophets to serve as His mouthpieces. Of them Peter writes, "Of this salvation the prophets have inquired and searched carefully, who prophesied of the grace that would come to you, searching what, or what manner of time, the Spirit of Christ who was in them was indicating when He testified beforehand the sufferings of Christ and the glories that would follow" (1 Peter 1:10–11).

Peter tells us that prophets did not speak of their own accord but were carried by the Spirit of Christ to preach and to write the words of God Himself. Peter describes something of the process in his second letter: "No prophecy of Scripture is of any private interpretation, for prophecy never came by the will of man, but holy men of God spoke as they were moved by the Holy Spirit" (2 Peter 1:20–21). These men of old knew what they were saying but they did not understand the fullness of it in respect to salvation.

Though angels inhabited the heavenly realm and were dispatched from God's side for a variety of purposes, they served God in the moment and did not have insider knowledge of such things. How marvelous it must have been when the angel Gabriel was sent to Mary and Joseph to bring the news! How joyous it must have been for the angel to announce to the shepherds the fulfillment of prophetic word in the birth of a Savior who is Christ the Lord, and to be joined by the angelic host in a chorus of praise!

That day longed for by the prophets and angels had come, and Peter was witness to it. He saw the suffering of Christ and the glory of His resurrection. He encountered the risen Christ and proclaimed the good news of the gospel in the power of the Holy Spirit poured out at Pentecost.

PRINCIPLE

What the prophets saw in shadow, we see in substance.
In what way does the Bible carry a single message?

Chapter 13

Gird Your Mind

"...gird up the loins of your mind..."
(1 Peter 1:13)

If you were going to build a house, where would you begin? Perhaps you'd start with the foundation. That solid footing is necessary for the stability and endurance of the structure. But actually, there is an even more foundational starting point. You would need plans. Those architectural plans would dictate the dimensions of the foundation and the specifications of the house rising from it.

Peter locates the starting point for Christian living as the mind. In the mind we spread out the blueprints of God's Word for our character and conduct, and we seek the Holy Spirit to guide us and strengthen us for the project. We determine whom we will follow—the living God or lifeless idols. We commit ourselves to seeking the kingdom of God and His righteousness. We set our sights on obedience in conformity to the will of God. We purpose to punctuate every aspect with the phrase, "in keeping with the will of our God." For the believer, the mind is the nerve center for the busy construction site that is the Christian life.

The most prominent word in the Greek New Testament for repentance has to do with the mind. From serving idols, we turn our faces to God in faith and repentance, pledging our allegiance and submitting our wills. From that reorientation of the mind, we bring forth fruit in keeping with repentance. We are to set our minds on things above where we are seated with Christ. We are renewed by the transforming of our mind. We take every thought captive to the obedience of Christ, a frontline challenge against the spiritual opposition we face in the building project to which we are assigned.

So it's no surprise that Peter instructs us to "gird up the loins of your mind, be sober, and rest your hope fully upon the grace that is to be brought to you at the revelation of Jesus Christ" (1 Peter 1:13). "Gird up" might sound strange to our ear but basically it has to do with preparation. We might think of steeling ourselves to receive bad news or readying ourselves for some endeavor such as a camping trip. The image is of rolling up our sleeves to get down to the task at hand.

Earlier, Peter reminded us that we were chosen for obedience and then went on to describe the glorious hope that is ours in Christ. Now he calls us to get down to the business of obedience, fueled by his words of courage and comfort. In so doing, we purpose to honor Christ in our beliefs and in our behavior. The Christian life is an intentional life. We must remain sober-minded, serious, and focused in the conduct of our lives, buoyed by the joy that is ours in Christ.

In so doing, Peter lifts our eyes to the horizon of our sojourning, calling us to focus particularly on the return of our Lord Jesus. There, we see a sure hope and an end to our longing and suffering. The grace that's brought us safe thus far is the grace that will bring us home. Ultimately, the building project belongs to our God. We are His workmanship. He who began a good work in us will indeed see it to completion.

PRINCIPLE

The Spirit renews us through the management of our mind.
How do we go about girding our minds for action?

Chapter 14

Well-Behaved Children

"Be holy, for I am holy."
(1 Peter 1:16)

When my wife and I were raising our four children, we required two nonnegotiable things of them: respect and obedience. We gave latitude and expression as our children matured but it was always tethered to those two basics. In respecting us, they were respecting God's provision for their direction and protection. Obedience meant that they would put into practice what they heard from us. Obedience goes along with being a child under parental authority.

Peter addresses us as "obedient children" (1:14). At the outset of his letter, Peter informed us that we were chosen for obedience (1:2). Now, after reminding us that we are heirs in Christ, he addresses us as obedient children. Peter reminds us of our relationship with God as our heavenly Father. We are heirs, having the rights and responsibilities of children of God.

Peter fleshes out this obedience in two ways. Negatively, he insists that we no longer live in a manner that characterized us prior to our conversion to Christ and the lusts that ruled us. Later, Peter will tell us: "For we have spent enough of our past lifetime in doing the will of the Gentiles—when we walked in lewdness, lusts, drunkenness, revelries, drinking parties, and abominable idolatries" (1 Peter 4:3). Positively, Peter urges us to live consistently with our new life in Christ, being "holy in all our conduct." This before-and-after paradigm is basic to Christian discipleship, inherent in our Lord's call to those who follow Him: "If anyone desires to come after Me, let him deny himself, and take up his cross daily, and follow Me" (Luke 9:23).

These before-and-after portrayals run throughout Peter's letters. Living out our newness in Christ brings glory to God and prompts others to see our good behavior and themselves give glory to our Father in heaven. Obedience is the natural and necessary outworking of our new birth by which we have been adopted into the family of God.

Peter will come at this call to obedience in a variety of ways throughout his writing, building his case that the gospel brings us not merely to a new status but also to a new manner of living. The apostle Paul adopted the same tact. "For you were once darkness, but now you are light in the Lord. Walk as children of light (for the fruit of the Spirit is in all goodness, righteousness, and truth)" (Eph. 5:8–9). We are light in the Lord; therefore, we are to be light. We are holy to God and to be holy as He, our heavenly Father, is holy (1 Peter 1:15–16).

That raises the question: How is our Father holy? How are we to emulate Him? We are to be set apart, internally and externally consistent with who we are in Christ (cf. 2 Peter 1:3–9). Growing in the knowledge of God will enable us to take hold of two things: a deeper understanding of holiness, and a more profound grasp of our absolute need for Jesus Christ.

PRINCIPLE

Our call to holiness in Christ exhibits itself in obedience to the Father. What exactly are we called to obey?

Chapter 15

Redeemed

*". . .conduct yourselves throughout the time of
your stay here in fear. . ."*
(1 Peter 1:17)

What comes to mind when you hear the word "gospel"? Paul
characterizes the gospel as righteousness from God that is
by faith in what Christ achieved, and not by works done by us. It
holds the promise of forgiveness of sins and life eternal. He pithily
captures the gospel in terms of the humiliation and exaltation of
the eternal Son of God incarnate in fulfillment of Old Testament
prophecy: "Remember that Jesus Christ, of the seed of David, was
raised from the dead according to my gospel" (2 Tim. 2:8).

But the gospel is more than Christ's redemption of a people and
salvation of the individual. The gospel of Christ's redeeming work
extends to the entire created order fallen under the scourge of sin.
As Paul put it, the creation groans along with us for the consum-
mation of the new creation (Rom. 8:22–23). That redemptive reality and realization give us our hope, something Peter will go on to
detail for us.

Jesus referred to the gospel as the "gospel of the kingdom" (Matt.
4:23). The kingdom referred both to Christ's deliverance and rule
(Col. 1:13–14). It was expressed in our Lord's teaching, illustrated
in His parables, and demonstrated in works of power that showed
authority over the rule of Satan and reversal of the effects of the
fall. For us to embrace the gospel is to recognize Christ as King. In
bowing before Him, we embrace Him as Lord of all. That means
we consider ourselves citizens of heaven and aliens in this world.

It is on that basis Peter urges us: "And if you call on the Father,
who without partiality judges according to each one's work, conduct yourselves throughout the time of your stay here in fear;

knowing that you were not redeemed with corruptible things, like silver or gold, from your aimless conduct received by tradition from your fathers, but with the precious blood of Christ, as of a lamb without blemish and without spot" (1 Peter 1:17–19). To know God as Father speaks to our redeemed relationship with Him but also to our being set apart for Him even though we find ourselves in this world for the moment. It's expected that when we pray to our Father who is in heaven that we would also pray that His will would be done and His kingdom would come on earth as it is in heaven.

A gospel-directed life speaks not only to the comfort and joy of our security in Christ but also to advancing His kingdom. It addresses both consolation and conduct. It flows out of a new heart taken captive by Christ to follow Him, serve Him, and honor Him in every facet, every role, every day, everywhere. A gospel-directed life is a Christ-centered life, dependent on Him, devoted to Him, designed by Him.

PRINCIPLE

The gospel is the gospel of the kingdom.
What does that mean for our status and our service?

Chapter 16

Manifest Destiny

". . .so that your faith and hope are in God."
(1 Peter 1:21)

The old gospel song, "Because He lives, we can face tomorrow," has a Petrine ring to it. Early on in his letter, Peter pointed us to the God and Father of our Lord Jesus and affirmed a living hope through the resurrection of Jesus Christ from the dead (1:3). Peter again brings that hope to bear and the difference it makes in our outlook and in the outworking of our lives.

Peter puts it that we are to "stay here in fear" (1:17). He is speaking of our time in the world that is not our home. That time is to be lived in fear. That does not mean we cower in the face of opposition or adversity. Rather, our lives are lived in awe of God and apprehension of His redemption of us. He reminds us that: "You were not redeemed with corruptible things, like silver or gold, from your aimless conduct received by tradition from your fathers, but with the precious blood of Christ, as of a lamb without blemish and without spot" (1 Peter 1:18–19).

We are holy in the Lord and to be holy in all we do. We conduct ourselves in the fear of the Lord, making a holy God our point of reference for our lives here as aliens and sojourners. But those efforts on our part are not the basis for our hope. Our hope rests in the work of the triune God and His sovereign accomplishment of salvation. Yet our efforts are descriptive of our hope, a hope that rests exclusively and fully on the work of Jesus Christ on the stage of human history. "He indeed was foreordained before the foundation of the world, but was manifest in these last times for you who through Him believe in God, who raised Him from the dead and gave Him glory, so that your faith and hope are in God" (1 Peter 1:20–21).

Echoing the language of the writer of Hebrews (Heb. 1:1–3), Peter speaks of the fullness of time when the mystery became manifest, shadow became substance, the anticipated became actualized. The sacrificial lambs of the Old Testament gave way to the Lamb of God who was both priest and offering in the accomplishment of the redemption they could only point to. We live because He lived and died and lives again.

Peter is making the connection between what we know and how we live. If you handle adversity with the idea of just hanging in there, trying your best, and toughing it out, you may well plod on through. But Peter speaks to us as children of God and lifts our eyes to Him and the wonders He has done in Christ on our behalf. Our hope is sure. Our faith has focus. Our conduct has purpose. Our suffering will end. Our God gives us strength for today and bright hope for tomorrow. He who did not spare His own Son, will He not in Him give us all things?

That perspective sanctifies our trials. It situates us in the arms of the God who loved us and gave His Son for us, the God who is with us to cheer and to guide. And one day, faith will be sight and what we see in shadow now will give way to the reality that cast it.

PRINCIPLE

Fear is the focus of faith that regards the hand of the living God. How does hope in the Lord relate to fear of the Lord?

Chapter 17

The Outworking of Love

". . .love one another fervently with a pure heart. . ."
(1 Peter 1:22)

Peter features prominently in the last chapter of John's Gospel. When His disciples had finished the breakfast prepared by the risen Christ, Jesus turned to Peter and asked him if he loved Him. Peter immediately affirmed his love. But Jesus asked the question again and Peter reaffirmed his love. When Jesus asked the question a third time, John records that Peter was grieved and responded emphatically that he loved Jesus.

Following each of these exchanges, Jesus gave Peter the charge to care for His sheep. What might our Lord's purpose have been in this exchange? Perhaps because Peter had denied Jesus three times, Jesus was giving him a threefold assurance of His continued purpose for him in building His church (Matt. 16:18–19). Though Peter had forsaken Jesus, Jesus had not forsaken him.

But why would Jesus test or highlight Peter's love for Him as a condition to care for His sheep? It's because love for Christ is the qualifier for loving Christ's sheep. Shepherds lead the flock by following Christ, who laid down His life for the sheep. At the close of his epistle, it is clear that Peter embraced his role to shepherd the flock in the name of the chief Shepherd (1 Peter 5:1–4). The very letter he writes is an expression of that shepherding.

Here in the first chapter of his letter, Peter issues a call for love as part of the family of God. While we might make several observations, the one most relevant at this stage of Peter's letter is that all of the blessings Peter has thus far described belong to a community. We are sheep who are part of a flock that has been redeemed by Christ. We are to be holy because God is holy (1 Peter 1:16) and we are incorporated into a holy nation (1 Peter

2:9). By God's grace and saving purpose, we are born again into the family of God.

We can see the community aspect in Peter's admonition. "Since you have purified your souls in obeying the truth through the Spirit in sincere love of the brethren, love one another fervently with a pure heart, having been born again, not of corruptible seed but incorruptible, through the word of God which lives and abides forever" (1 Peter 1:22–23). Earlier Peter called us to love Jesus, though we have not seen Him with our physical eyes as had Peter. Now that love for Jesus is to spread throughout the community of faith.

Peter will explain what it looks like to love in this community of God's love, but for now he simply urges us to love one another from the heart. He uses words to qualify our love—*sincerely, earnestly,* and *eager.* Each of these terms becomes for us a gauge by which we measure the quality of our love for our brothers and sisters in Christ. We love Him who first loved us and we love those He loves.

PRINCIPLE

Truth begets love when centered on Christ.
How can you assess the strength of your love for the brethren?

Chapter 18

The Living Word

"But the word of the LORD endures forever."
(1 Peter 1:25)

Peter held a high view of the Bible. He regarded it for what it is, the Word of God Himself. In his second epistle, Peter explains to us the nature of Scripture: "No prophecy of Scripture is of any private interpretation, for prophecy never came by the will of man, but holy men of God spoke as they were moved by the Holy Spirit" (2 Peter 1:20–21). In other words, men wrote the Bible but they did so as they were borne along by the Holy Spirit. The human authors of Scripture used their intellect, experiences, and styles to write what they did but that writing was superintended by the Spirit of God so that it is holy, inspired, inerrant, and infallible. Just as Peter recognized that Paul's letters were included as part of the New Testament canon (2 Peter 3:15–16), no doubt he realized that was the case with his own apostolic writing.

In affirming the authorship of man but authority of the Holy Spirit, Peter recognizes that the written Word does not ultimately originate with man but with God. The Spirit inspires, illuminates, and accomplishes His purposes through the Bible, both the Old Testament and the New. God has given us His Word, in writing—what Peter describes as living and abiding (1:23).

More than being a recorded historical account or a collection of stories and heroic exploits, or a compilation of spiritual maxims, the Bible throughout features God's Savior and holds the power of God to know and receive Him. After calling Scripture living and abiding, Peter cites Isaiah 40, saying, "All flesh is as grass, and all the glory of man as the flower of the grass. The grass withers, and its flower falls away, but the word of the LORD endures forever" (1 Peter 1:24–25). This Word is enduring, living and active, sharper than any two-edged sword, piercing to the thoughts and intentions of the heart (Heb. 4:12). It accomplishes the purposes for which God intends it (Isa. 55:11), both in history and in our lives.

Peter punctuates the power and purpose of the Word when he says, "Now this is the word which by the gospel was preached to you" (1 Peter 1:25). The beating heart of the Scriptures is the good news of salvation bound up in Jesus Christ, something Peter has summarized (1 Peter 1:20–21), characterized (1 Peter 1:24–25), and shown to be God's means (1 Peter 1:23) for the accomplishment of God's saving purposes. Peter would recall the insistence of Jesus when He said: "I did not come to destroy but to fulfill. For assuredly, I say to you, till heaven and earth pass away, one jot or one tittle will by no means pass from the law till all is fulfilled" (Matt. 5:18). Every expression of God's Word finds fulfillment in Jesus Christ (John 5:39; Luke 24:44–48).

All this serves as a reminder for us of what we possess in the Holy Scriptures. Through them, the Spirit reveals the mind of God, displays His glory, introduces His Messiah, nourishes our soul with the truth, and invigorates us for our journey as aliens and sojourners.

PRINCIPLE

The Bible is the living Word of the living God displaying the living Savior for a living hope.
How regularly do we spend time with God in His Word?

Chapter 19

Pure Spiritual Milk

". . .as newborn babes, desire the pure milk of the word. . ."
(1 Peter 2:2)

One of my favorite memories as a parent was of my wife sitting in the rocker in our nursery holding a crying baby as he or she rooted in to latch on to nurse. Loud cries of hunger settled down to whimpers of anticipation and finally to coos of contentment.

Peter brings that image to bear when he speaks of our maturation as babes in Christ: "As newborn babes, desire the pure milk of the word, that you may grow thereby" (1 Peter 2:2). Babies don't reason that way. They don't go through the mental process of thinking that if they eat well they will grow. Peter, however, appeals to our will, urging us to drink deeply of what God has provided for our spiritual development. He wants us to cultivate that desire.

When the writer of Hebrews speaks of spiritual milk, he contrasts it with solid food. "For though by this time you ought to be teachers, you need someone to teach you again the first principles of the oracles of God; and you have come to need milk and not solid food" (Heb. 5:12). Peter, however, is not admonishing us for lack of maturity. He is urging us to proper nourishment that will prompt our growth in the grace and knowledge of our Lord Jesus Christ.

Peter identifies two things related to our partaking. One, have we experienced new birth in Christ (1 Peter 1:23)? Have we indeed tasted that the Lord is good (1 Peter 2:3)? Has God worked His saving grace in our hearts that we might declare with spiritual sense and sensibility a newfound delight in God? With the new birth comes an appetite for God's Word. One theologian says that a hunger for Scriptural truth is the first indication of new life in Christ. What was tasteless or even repugnant to us when we were dead in sin now becomes savory and desirable. We can relate to the description of the psalmist in respect to God's precepts: "More to be desired are they than gold, yea, than much fine gold; sweeter also than honey and the honeycomb" (Ps. 19:10). God's Word is sweet to our taste, nourishing to our souls, and enlivening in our weariness.

The other thing Peter brings to bear related to our partaking of the milk of God's Word is its purity. I remember visiting a dairy farm many years ago. The milk from the cows was being loaded into a tanker truck. What I saw was surprising. It was filled with all sorts of impurities. It was nothing like what I was used to purchasing from the grocery store. The dairy farmer explained that it had not yet been processed.

The milk of Scripture comes to us pure. Yet it can be adulterated with contaminants of error or the impurities of malice, deceit, envy, or evil. Teaching of the world can be added to it, corrupting it, watering it down, and even poisoning it by twisting it to mean other than what God says. It's no wonder the last book of the Bible warns against adding to it or taking away from it (Rev. 22:18–19). Our spiritual growth comes from a steady diet of God's unadulterated Word, made effectual through His Spirit.

PRINCIPLE

God's Word is like a mother's milk, providing nourishment to grow and immunities to protect against spiritual harm. How can we cultivate our desire for God's Word?

Chapter 20

Living Stones

"Coming to Him as to a living stone, rejected indeed by men, but chosen by God and precious. . ."
(1 Peter 2:4)

B oth Peter and Paul refer to the community of God's people as a building. Paul writes to the church at Ephesus, saying that they are "members of the household of God, having been built on the foundation of the apostles and prophets, Jesus Christ Himself being the chief cornerstone, in whom the whole building, being fitted together, grows into a holy temple in the Lord, in whom you also are being built together for a dwelling place of God in the Spirit" (Eph. 2:19–22). Now Peter says that "you also, as living stones, are being built up a spiritual house (1 Peter 2:5).

That thought jars us a bit because we are often quick to emphasize that the church is not a building; it is people. A building is merely brick and mortar, something that can be raised up or torn down, or, as we often see nowadays, repurposed. We see buildings that once housed a congregation now being used for office space, college classrooms, or a pub, or simply abandoned and falling apart.

Yet that cannot happen with us as part of God's spiritual house. We are living stones, so called because we are united to Jesus Christ. As Peter puts it, we come "to Him as to a living stone, rejected indeed by men, but chosen by God and precious" (1 Peter 2:4). That's why Paul can speak of a building growing. He's not talking about multiple additions like we might add an education wing to our facility. He's speaking of God's workmanship of grace that adds daily to those being saved.

Peter brings to bear the work of God described in the Old Testament and fulfilled in the New. He quotes from the prophet Isaiah to say: "Behold, I lay in Zion a chief cornerstone, elect, precious, and he who believes on Him will by no means be put to shame" (1 Peter 2:6). God has one church, His chosen ones that span history and geography, enfolded into the community of faith in God's Messiah. All those who trust in Him will be saved. Those who refuse to believe will find themselves outside the house of God and perish. It all depends on our relationship to Christ: "Therefore, to you who believe, He is precious; but to those who are disobedient, 'The stone which the builders rejected has become the chief cornerstone'" (1 Peter 2:7).

Peter is reminding us here what he proclaimed before the religious leaders of his day. "This is the 'stone which was rejected by you builders, which has become the chief cornerstone.' Nor is there salvation in any other, for there is no other name under heaven given among men by which we must be saved" (Acts 4:11–12). Through His apostle, God is calling us to recognize Jesus Christ as the Messiah, that He is the fulfillment of Old Testament promise, and that salvation is gained only by faith in Him.

In God's household we function as priests, each of us, not only pastors, not just elders, but every one of us. "You also, as living stones, are being built up a spiritual house, a holy priesthood, to offer up spiritual sacrifices acceptable to God through Jesus Christ" (1 Peter 2:5). Peter will go on to explain more about our role as priests, but here we are reminded that the spiritual house God is building includes us and involves us in a holy calling.

PRINCIPLE

We are Christ's church.
What does it mean that we are living stones,
and how do we function as priests?

Chapter 21

God's Peculiar People

"But you are. . . His own special people. . ."
(1 Peter 2:9)

God's central promise that runs throughout Scripture is that
He would be God to His chosen people and they would be
His children. Peter seizes on this promise in his message to the
people gathered in Jerusalem for Pentecost. "Repent, and let every
one of you be baptized in the name of Jesus Christ for the remis-
sion of sins; and you shall receive the gift of the Holy Spirit. For
the promise is to you and to your children, and to all who are afar
off, as many as the Lord our God will call" (Acts 2:38–39). As the
promise of blessing was to believers and their children under the
old covenant, so the promise of blessing is to believers and their
children under the new covenant.

Now, Peter brings to bear descriptions that belonged to ancient
Israel and applies them to all the people of God, all those He pur-
posed to belong to Him. Peter declares those bound up by faith
in God's Messiah to be "a chosen generation, a royal priesthood,
a holy nation, His own special people" (1 Peter 2:9). He borrows
this description from Old Testament passages like Exodus 19:5–6:
" 'Now therefore, if you will indeed obey My voice and keep My
covenant, then you shall be a special treasure to Me above all
people; for all the earth is Mine. And you shall be to Me a kingdom
of priests and a holy nation.' These are the words which you shall
speak to the children of Israel." Peter reminds us that there is one
way of salvation and one people of God (cf. Heb. 11:39–40).

Peter reinforces our bond with the saints of old by applying to us
on this side of the cross God's Word from the prophet Hosea. We
"who once were not a people but are now the people of God, who
had not obtained mercy but now have obtained mercy" (1 Peter

2:10). We stand as we do only by the grace of God, not because we are choice but because we are chosen, "elect according to the fore-knowledge of God" (1 Peter 1:2). Paul applies this same passage after saying, "that He might make known the riches of His glory on the vessels of mercy, which He had prepared beforehand for glory, even us whom He called, not of the Jews only, but also of the Gentiles" (Rom. 9:23–24). As sinners saved by grace, we have standing before a holy God not owed to anything worthy in us but, on the contrary, only because of the mercy of God set upon us.

In light of such love, what is our calling? Peter lays it out for us: "That you may proclaim the praises of Him who called you out of darkness into His marvelous light" (1 Peter 2:9). How do we do that? How do we make such proclamation? We do it by living in a manner worthy of our calling in Christ, something Peter will go on to emphasize. We do it in the context of corporate worship, where we gather to rehearse the grandeur of our God and the glories of the gospel. We do it in our witness to those still in darkness, something we see exhibited by Peter in the book of Acts and expected of us in our personal mission fields (1 Peter 3:15). God's praise is to echo in our hearts and stand poised on our lips.

PRINCIPLE

God has tuned our hearts to sing His praise.
What might be the subjects of the stanzas of our song?

Chapter 22

A Living Epistle

". . .that. . . they may, by your good works which they observe,
glorify God in the day of visitation."
(1 Peter 2:12)

Perhaps you've heard the exhortation to "preach the gospel at all times and if necessary use words." That has a nice ring to it, particularly when so many professing believers live contrary to the faith they profess, saying one thing but doing another. There is something appealing and authentic about being living epistles, reflecting Christ in us, the hope of glory. Plus, it accords with our Lord's teaching from the Sermon on the Mount: "Let your light so shine before men, that they may see your good works and glorify your Father in heaven" (Matt. 5:16).

The problem with this exhortation, however, is that it is unbiblical, or at best does not reflect the whole of biblical teaching. It is true that we are to live as light in darkness. Peter has admonished us to comport ourselves in a manner consistent with our calling and conspicuous for Christ. The way we conduct ourselves distinguishes us from those without God and without hope in this world, and may well provoke inquiry from those who take notice (cf. 1 Peter 3:15).

Here in chapter two, Peter has addressed us as a royal priesthood, a people belonging to God, loved by Him. He urges us to abstain from evil and devote ourselves to our kingdom allegiance and obedience under the lordship of Jesus Christ, with an eye to provoking glory to God in the eyes of others. "Beloved, I beg you as sojourners and pilgrims, abstain from fleshly lusts which war against the soul, having your conduct honorable among the Gentiles, that when they speak against you as evildoers, they may, by your good works which they observe, glorify God in the day of visitation" (1 Peter 2:11–12).

While our behavior may indeed stimulate interest, those good works cannot stand by themselves as witness. If we witness without words, we point to ourselves—how great we are instead of how great God is. If we allow our example to witness for us, we communicate another gospel, salvation by works rather than by grace alone. And where will Christ fit in to the picture we display unless we lift Him up as the Savior of sinners and Lord of life? Only by explaining our behavior in terms of Christ and the gospel will God be glorified on the day of visitation.

But our conduct is important. It is our calling card to a world shrouded in the darkness of sin. Peter urges us not to conform to the world in its rebellion against God by adopting its values, priorities, and practices. Nor are we to be taken captive by our desires, as our enemy the devil would entice us. Rather, we are to wage war. On the one hand, Peter calls us to abstain from fleshly lusts. On the other, we are to keep our conduct honorable. Our aim is not to exalt ourselves but to exhibit Christ.

PRINCIPLE

Our witness moves forward on the two feet of word and deed.
How can you have a more pronounced impact for Christ
on others?

Chapter 23

Honor the Emperor

". . .submit yourselves to every ordinance of man for
the Lord's sake. . ."
(1 Peter 2:13)

Our Lord Jesus made it clear in His high priestly prayer (John 17) that His disciples are in the world but not of the world. Peter has reflected that duality by indicating we live in this world but we do so as aliens and sojourners. We live here on mission as ambassadors of our King. Peter has just written about living our lives as citizens of heaven. With that comes the mandate to live expressly under the lordship of Christ, conducting ourselves in a manner that honors Him and bears witness to others among whom we live in this world.

That means honoring the institutions God has ordained. Peter writes: "Therefore submit yourselves to every ordinance of man for the Lord's sake, whether to the king as supreme, or to governors, as to those who are sent by him for the punishment of evildoers and for the praise of those who do good" (1 Peter 2:13–14). As believers, we are to recognize and respect the order and authority of government.

When Peter and Jesus were in Capernaum, a tax collector approached Peter and asked if Jesus paid temple tax (Matt. 17:24–27). This question was a trap of sorts in that His enemies were trying to pit Jesus against governmental authorities. In His response, Jesus honored God and the king. His kingdom was not of this world but that did not mean that His subjects were to disregard the authority of God-ordained government. As our Lord put it elsewhere, "Render therefore to Caesar the things that are Caesar's, and to God the things that are God's" (Matt. 22:21). Of course, all things belong to God and are under His authority, including human government (John 19:11; Rom. 13:1–7).

In calling us to submit to civil authority, Peter brings to bear those same themes emphasized by Jesus. "For this is the will of God, that by doing good you may put to silence the ignorance of foolish men—as free, yet not using liberty as a cloak for vice, but as bondservants of God. Honor all people. Love the brotherhood. Fear God. Honor the king" (1 Peter 2:15–17). Our subjection honors God and His design for civil order and bears witness to our ultimate submission to the King of kings before the eyes of others.

When Peter calls us to live as free, he qualifies that freedom not as license to sin but as incentive to live for God. That's why when confronted with demands contrary to the will of God, Peter defiantly and definitively declared: "We must obey God rather than men" (Acts 5:29, ESV). In our society today, we are confronted with many options for evil. We cannot use our freedom as occasion for sin. There are societally sanctioned options that are improper for God's holy people, to which we must say, "No thanks." But it may come that these options will be imposed upon us under threat, to which we must say, "No way!" and be ready to suffer for righteousness' sake as Peter described for us.

PRINCIPLE

*Our freedom in Christ is to promote neither
license nor lawlessness.
What is the Christian's relationship to civil authority?*

Chapter 24

Suffering for Good

"But when you do good and suffer, if you take it patiently, this is
commendable before God."
(1 Peter 2:20)

When Peter and the other apostles were told by religious authorities not to teach in the name of Jesus, they answered according to a higher authority when they declared, "We must obey God rather than men" (Acts 5:29). And they suffered the consequences. We're told that the leaders were enraged and wanted to kill them. In His providence God spared their lives, but they did end up being beaten and told again not to teach in the name of Jesus. The apostles' response? "So they departed from the presence of the council, rejoicing that they were counted worthy to suffer shame for His name. And daily in the temple, and in every house, they did not cease teaching and preaching Jesus as the Christ" (Acts 5:41–42). In other words, they endured anguish while suffering unjustly, and found joy in so doing.

In his letter, Peter has called us to live our lives in this world as becomes followers of Christ. That lifestyle of love and righteousness reflects the kingdom to which we belong, having been enfolded into it by the grace and power of God. We bring glory to God and bring witness to the world in which we sojourn. That allegiance relates to every aspect of our lives, whether as citizens, workers, family members, or to whatever human institution God has designed for the ordering and well-being of society, even if that institution has been corrupted by sin.

After calling us to submit to civil government, Peter addresses servants (v. 18). Here he speaks to those who have the job of a domestic servant in a household, who, as servants of God, are to serve their masters well. It is an application of honoring those in authority (v. 17), and not only those who rule honorably but even those who are inconsiderate and unkind. "We are to show respect not only to the good and gentle, but also to the harsh" (1 Peter 2:18). We are to serve well for the sake of Christ, whom we ultimately serve.

Under the rule of Christ, we operate on different principles than those of the world. We are mindful that we do our work not primarily for men but for the Lord. We do not treat people as they deserve but by grace. We are willing to suffer wrong and injustice. Peter brings to bear the principle he exhibited when treated unjustly. "For this is commendable, if because of conscience toward God one endures grief, suffering wrongfully. For what credit is it if, when you are beaten for your faults, you take it patiently? But when you do good and suffer, if you take it patiently, this is commendable before God" (1 Peter 2:19–20).

Patiently persevering in the face of suffering, even if that suffering is unjust, is a hallmark of the Christian. It is exhibited by our Lord and expected of us as His disciples. Unfair suffering is counterintuitive in our rights-oriented society, particularly nowadays when any sort of mistreatment or inconvenience or injustice warrants formal grievance or legal action. But Christ's kingdom is countercultural. We are to love our enemies and bless those who mistreat us, knowing that our reward transcends a paycheck or promotion, but is administered by our Father in heaven.

PRINCIPLE

Our treatment of others is to reflect God's treatment of us.
How does your attitude toward the other political party
need to change?

Chapter 25

Called to Suffer

*"For to this you were called, because Christ also suffered for us,
leaving us an example, that you should follow His steps. . ."*
(1 Peter 2:21)

"For to this you were called." That's how Peter begins verse 21 as he lifts our eyes to the Lord Jesus. So much of the Christian life relates to and revolves around our calling. That's the case with Peter. In Matthew's Gospel account, Jesus declares to a professing Peter that on the rock of his profession of Jesus as the Christ, the Son of the living God, Jesus would build His church (Matt. 16:13–18). Jesus also issues a general call to those who would follow Him. "If anyone desires to come after Me, let him deny himself, and take up his cross, and follow Me" (Matt. 16:24). The Christian is called to die to self and live for Christ. Paul captures the theme not only of his epistles but of the whole of Scripture: "I, therefore, the prisoner of the Lord, beseech you to walk worthy of the calling with which you were called" (Eph. 4:1; Ps. 147:19–20).

Now Peter invokes our call. What is the "this" to which we are called that Peter highlights? Clearly, it is suffering unjustly, suffering for righteousness' sake, suffering in the model of our Lord Jesus Christ. It is part and parcel of denying ourselves and taking up our cross, signifying suffering and death, to follow Jesus as His disciples. Jesus is our pattern. "For to this you were called, because Christ also suffered for us, leaving us an example, that you should follow His steps" (1 Peter 2:21).

Jesus is the epitome of suffering unjustly. He neither acted with sin nor reacted in sin. Peter tells us: He "committed no sin, nor was deceit found in His mouth; who, when He was reviled, did not revile in return; when He suffered, He did not threaten" (1 Peter 2:22–23). On the one hand, Jesus suffered by virtue of His humiliation, the Creator taking on humanity so that He might take to Himself the guilt of our sin. In that model, we suffer as ones in the world but not of it, fish out of water as pilgrims awaiting heavenly glory. On the other hand, Jesus suffered at the hands of sinful men. We, too, suffer in this manner as our light shines in the darkness and the darkness does not like it. Like Christ, let us suffer not because we deserve it but for righteousness' sake.

What do we do when we are provoked, particularly when we know we are in the right? Often, we will lash out. But no one had the higher moral ground more than Jesus, yet He did not respond in kind. What did Jesus do when unjustly provoked? Peter tells us that He "committed Himself to Him who judges righteously" (1 Peter 2:23). Paul echoes the same thought: "Beloved, do not avenge yourselves, but rather give place to wrath; for it is written, 'Vengeance is Mine, I will repay,' says the Lord" (Rom. 12:19).

Jesus is more than our example, as Peter will explain to us in a moment, but He is not less. Suffering is part and parcel of our call, a nail Peter will continue to hit on the head through the remainder of his letter. He will go so far as to say that we share in Christ's sufferings (4:13), much as he and the others did at the hands of their persecutors (Acts 5:41).

PRINCIPLE

Jesus shows us how to suffer unjustly.
How does your treatment of others reflect
your relationship with Jesus?

Chapter 26

Unlike Jesus

". . .who Himself bore our sins in His own body on the tree. . ."
(1 Peter 2:24)

WWJD poses a legitimate question for those who count themselves disciples and seek to emulate their Lord. *What would Jesus do?* It's a natural and necessary question for those who belong to the kingdom of God. What ambitions, attitudes, activities, and priorities should characterize us? We begin our answer by looking to Jesus. As Peter has just reminded us regarding suffering, our Lord Jesus suffered for us, leaving us an example, that we might follow in His steps (2:21).

There are those ways, however, where we are not expected to be like Jesus and indeed we cannot be. Peter goes on to say that Jesus "Himself bore our sins in His own body on the tree, that we, having died to sins, might live for righteousness—by whose stripes you were healed" (1 Peter 2:24). Christ alone atoned for sin. While we are to die to sin and live for righteousness, we are in no way acting as a substitute, representing others as did our Lord Jesus. Our suffering for righteousness' sake merits nothing, certainly not for others but not even for ourselves. Jesus paid it all.

It is by Christ's redeeming work that we have been freed from sin's penalty and from sin's power, and will one day be freed from sin's presence. As Peter puts it, it is by His wounds that we have been healed. We experience a measure of that healing now and will one day experience it in forever fullness.

Our pursuit of righteousness is a reflection of our newness in Christ and reorientation to life. "For you were like sheep going astray, but have now returned to the Shepherd and Overseer of your souls" (1 Peter 2:25). Our lives in Christ demonstrate a before and an after, a then and a now. We were straying, going our own way, lost and alone, but by God's pursuing grace we have returned not merely to safety but to Him who laid down His life for us and who watches over us. We have returned, as Peter puts it, because Christ retrieved us. We are back where we belong in communion with the God we were created to glorify and enjoy.

In this description of straying sheep Peter invokes the prophet Isaiah. "But He was wounded for our transgressions, He was bruised for our iniquities; the chastisement for our peace was upon Him, and by His stripes we are healed. All we like sheep have gone astray; we have turned, every one, to his own way; and the LORD has laid on Him the iniquity of us all" (Isa. 53:5–6). This eighth century BC preview of God's Suffering Servant to come reveals that we have returned because we were redeemed. Christ bore our sin and reconciled us to God. The "tree" to which Peter refers (2:24) is the cross of Calvary, where it pleased the Father to inflict a suffering upon Him beyond our comprehension (Isa. 53:10) because of a love we can never fully fathom (Rom. 5:6–11; Eph. 3:18–19).

PRINCIPLE

By Christ's example we are led but by His work we are saved.
What is your story of coming to Christ in the gospel?

Chapter 27

A Word to the Wives

"Wives, likewise, be submissive to your own husbands. . ."
(1 Peter 3:1)

Peter now turns his attention to wives. His address begins with the word "likewise." That means his admonition is connected to what he has already stated. It's like saying, "Your brother has to clean his room thoroughly. Likewise, you have to clean yours as well."

To what is Peter's word to the wives connected? If we look back at verse 19 of chapter 2, we see that Peter addressed servants, urging them to be subject to their masters. But even further back, we see Peter urging those who are Christians to be subject for the Lord's sake to every human institution, and then references kings and governors specifically (2:13). If we look ahead, we find Peter addressing husbands (3:7), and then "finally, all of you" (3:8). Peter is telling us that whatever role we assume and whatever task we undertake, we are to carry it out unto the Lord. The lordship of Jesus Christ governs the entirety of our lives, even in situations where our submission might lead to suffering.

In these relationships, Peter is urging us to kingdom conduct in the way we carry ourselves in this world as sojourners and pilgrims. As he has stressed, our being holy unto the Lord means we are wholly devoted to Him. Our primary concern is that our actions honor our Lord Jesus Christ. Secondarily, Peter will remind us that our kingdom conduct may well provoke those we encounter to ask us why we live as we do (3:15), and so give us opportunity to bear witness to Christ and the gospel. The expectation of exemplary conduct is not diminished because we might suffer for it or because those in authority over us are not deserving of it.

As he did with citizens and with servants, Peter focuses on

character and *conduct,* in this case, of wives in respect to their husbands. The beauty Peter calls for in wives is not mere outward or cosmetic, but inward and substantive. Their attractiveness is to "be the hidden person of the heart, with the incorruptible beauty of a gentle and quiet spirit, which is very precious in the sight of God" (1 Peter 3:4–5). God's concern for all of us is not external religious conformity but a heart that seeks and serves Him. Our culture may be concerned with certain standards of beauty but the beauty God desires is imperishable and will not wrinkle or wither.

Peter's main concern in this section is the adornment of the godly woman for the advancement of the gospel. A hallmark of the beauty God desires for wives is submission to their husbands (v. 5) as a tool for evangelism, out of concern for their souls. That's how Peter began his address: "Wives, likewise, be submissive to your own husbands, that even if some do not obey the word, they, without a word, may be won by the conduct of their wives" (1 Peter 3:1). In other words, despite their husbands' unbelief, wives focus on expressing the beauty of their own attitudes and actions and entrusting themselves to God for His mercy to their husbands. These godly women are illustrations of sacrifice and suffering for the sake of Christ.

PRINCIPLE

Man looks on the outward appearance but God knows the heart.
What is your standard for beauty?

Chapter 28

Husbands, Likewise

"Husbands, likewise. . ."
(1 Peter 3:7)

God has designed an ordered society for the well-being and prospering of mankind. That well-being is under severe threat in our day from rejection of gender and lifelong marriage between one man and one woman. Ultimately, that rejection is rebellion against God (Matt. 19:4–6).

Part of God's order involves structure and authority. We see it in the state, in the church, and in the home. In each of these spheres today, the creature is rising up against the Creator, declaring self-rule, to the extent that individual rights are evolving into individual realities. Peter has urged us as Christians, a holy priesthood, to "be subject for the Lord's sake to every human institution" (1 Peter 2:13). As God has given order to society, so has He to the church and the home. While the instruction to servants (2:19) has application to the workplace (cf. Col. 3:22), the term Peter uses addresses domestic servants of a household, hence the home. God wants us to recognize the roles we play and serve Him with our very best in those positions.

Peter has just addressed wives, calling them to cultivate an attractiveness not promoted on a billboard but an inner beauty found in the Bible, the glamour of godliness. In many ways, the wife is the model for the unity Peter will call all of us to in a moment (3:8–12). Now Peter turns to address husbands. He doesn't urge them to lord authority over their wives but to live in deference to them, sensitive to them. The wife is not an accessory to the husband as though she were of less importance or value. Peter emphasizes that wives are co-heirs of the grace of life. "Husbands, likewise, dwell with them with understanding, giving honor to the wife, as to the weaker vessel, and as being heirs together of the grace of life" (1 Peter 3:7). They are fellow sojourners together by the blessing of God, and fellow servants in honoring God's kingdom call.

Paul, in speaking of the structure of the home, also speaks of the tender honor that a husband is to give his wife. Husbands are to love their wives as Christ loved the church and gave Himself for her. They are to serve their wives in the model of Christ. To borrow from what Peter will later say about elders, husbands are to exercise oversight of their wives, not domineering over them, but being examples to them in loving humility.

Peter appends a reason for this posture of the husband to his wife: ". . . that your prayers may not be hindered" (3:7). By this, he is saying that the husband has a priestly function in the home and is to be fervent in prayer for those under his care, displaying sacrifice, sensitivity, and shepherding in the model of Christ.

In our day, this notion of roles in the home is deemed archaic, and the church is complicit in this demise. Rather than holding up Christ and a biblical model of serving one another as fellow heirs and partners in ministry, the church has embraced and enforced cultural stereotypes that overshadow God's design. The result has been throwing the baby of role differences out with the bathwater of cultural stereotypes.

PRINCIPLE

Christ must be the center of the heart and the home.
How can you best serve Christ in your home?

Chapter 29

Single-minded

"Finally, all of you be of one mind,
having compassion for one another. . ."
(1 Peter 3:8)

Love permeates the Christian life. The two great command-ments direct us to love God with the entirety of our being and our neighbor as ourselves. We are even called to love our enemies.

A "friend" I follow online asserted she did not and would not love her enemy. Since she considered herself a Christian, I made a rare comment in her feed with an eye to showing her that the command to love our enemies came from the mouth of Christ Himself. I wrote: "Jesus, who gave His life for His enemies (Romans 5:8–9), gives us practical ways to love our enemies. 'But I tell you who hear me: Love your enemies, do good to those who hate you, bless those who curse you, pray for those who mistreat you' (Luke 6:27–28)." Unfazed and sticking to her prideful guns, she responded: "Yeah, with all due respect to the Lord, no. I'm Italian." My friend showed her true colors and kingdom allegiance in flouting the One she acknowledges as lord in name only.

As an apostle of Jesus Christ, Peter looks each of us in the eye and says: "Finally, all of you be of one mind, having compassion for one another; love as brothers, be tenderhearted, be courteous; not return-ing evil for evil or reviling for reviling, but on the contrary blessing, knowing that you were called to this, that you may inherit a blessing" (1 Peter 3:8–9). Each of these facets can be traced in Scripture to the call to love. Sympathy, compassion, caring, humility, blessing—all flow from love of God and neighbor. Love is never theoretically defined in the Bible but is operationally defined. Peter's description here sounds much like the descriptions of 1 Corinthians 13 and Romans 12:9–21 with their practical emphases.

This multifaceted gem of God's grace stems from being "of one mind" (v. 8). That does not mean that we can't have differences of opinion but it does mean that we have a singleness of focus as followers of Jesus Christ. Early on in his letter, Peter told us to gird our minds for action by setting our hope fully and exclusively on the grace that is ours in Christ, from which our lives will flow out in loving obedience to Him who first loved us (1:13–14). Paul takes the same tack when he calls us to live out our new life in Christ. We are to set our minds on our position in Christ (Col. 3:1–3), from which flow new obedience and grace-filled community (Col. 3:12–17).

Basically, Peter wants us to see ourselves in a whole new light. We are no longer rebels, no longer autonomous, no longer isolated, no longer in it for ourselves. Kingdom decorum and desire center on Jesus. We lay our rights at His feet. We define our realities from His Word. In a moment, Peter will tell us to "sanctify the Lord in our hearts" (3:15). From that wellspring will flow living water to satisfy our longings, sustain us for the arduous journey, and stimulate us for gospel proclamation. And it all begins by being single-minded together in submission to our Lord.

PRINCIPLE

Love is not expressed in vague niceties but in practical terms.
In what ways can you practice love for others?

Chapter 30

Pursuing Peace

". . .seek peace and pursue it."
(1 Peter 3:11)

Conflict seems the norm in our day. On the political landscape, few are willing to seek common ground if the opposing party is there. Like an uncivil war, factions are at odds with each other when they should be united by a common country and a common cause. Society in general finds itself enraged, the fires of discord fanned by the flames of social media. Churches are being split apart, seemingly incapable of handling even the smallest of differences. Seething, isolation, and entrenchment feed into a divisiveness for which there seems no remedy.

But there is something we as God's people can do. We can be peacemakers. As far as it concerns us, we can purpose to live at peace with others, not contributing to conflict but de-escalating it when we can. Peter has pointed us to Jesus who, when reviled, did not revile in return (2:23). He has instructed us not to repay evil for evil or reviling for reviling (3:9).

Now Peter lays before us a plan for how we can be peacemakers. Quoting Psalm 34, he says: "He who would love life and see good days, let him refrain his tongue from evil, and his lips from speaking deceit. Let him turn away from evil and do good; let him seek peace and pursue it" (1 Peter 3:10–11). I think we can safely say that the conflict and ill-will we experience in our day generate angst in our own souls and in society as a whole. We long for the love of life and good days Peter holds up to us. Psalm 34 lays out a master plan for how we can pursue that state of being. It speaks of blessing the Lord at all times, of rejoicing in Him, and inviting others to join with us (Ps. 34:1–3). It directs us in crying out to the God who is attentive to our plea and who will hear and deliver us from our troubles (Ps. 34:4–6, 15, 17). It teaches us the posture for such prayer: "The LORD is near to those who have a broken heart, and saves such as have a contrite spirit" (Ps. 34:18).

Peter's excerpt from Psalm 34 focuses on our responsibility as peacemakers. What can we do in the name of Jesus to take the wind out of the sails of conflict? First, we must be careful not to pour gas on the flame through our words. How easy it is through sarcasm, caustic speech, and inflammatory language to make things worse! James issues severe warning about the tongue, speaking of it as "an unruly evil, full of deadly poison" (James 3:8) and capable of great destruction (James 3:5–6). Second, we must seek to build up and not tear down, asking ourselves what good can we do and how we can promote peace.

While we can work at being peacemakers, only God can work at the level of the heart. Only He can bring about healing from division. That's why Peter includes in his excerpt from Psalm 34 this hope: "For the eyes of the LORD are on the righteous, and His ears are open to their prayers; but the face of the LORD is against those who do evil" (1 Peter 3:12). We must pray for peace wherever the rupture of sin is found.

PRINCIPLE

Jesus brings peace on earth.
How can we contribute to peacemaking rather than
troublemaking?

Chapter 31

A Holy Defense

*"But sanctify the Lord God in your hearts, and always be ready to
give a defense to everyone who asks. . ."*
(1 Peter 3:15)

As I stood peering down at the unobtrusive street marker in
Oxford, England, it struck me as a portal to history. It's where
in 1555 men known as the Oxford Martyrs had been burned at
the stake for refusal to compromise their faith. Often war memorials are grand and sprawling, such as those in Washington DC that
commemorate the various conflicts in which the United States has
been engaged. But the Oxford Martyr marker, with its subtlety and
simplicity, is much more apt for the spiritual battle we wage for
the kingdom of Jesus Christ. The epitaph scribed by the writer of
Hebrews for stalwarts of the faith springs to mind—"of whom the
world was not worthy" (Heb. 11:38).

The apostle Peter knew something of what it meant to take such
a stand. He who had cowardly denied Jesus three times would go
on to display boldness and courage for the sake of Christ in the
face of opposition and persecution. The book of Acts records Peter
being threatened and beaten for the faith. Peter, however, saw these
confrontations as occasions to bear witness to the gospel (e.g., Acts
4:8–12; 5:29–32).

Peter urges us in the same manner. "And who is he who will
harm you if you become followers of what is good? But even if you
should suffer for righteousness' sake, you are blessed. 'And do not
be afraid of their threats, nor be troubled'" (1 Peter 3:13–14). The
apostle's words bring to mind our Lord's teaching in the Sermon on
the Mount: "Blessed are you when they revile and persecute you,
and say all kinds of evil against you falsely for My sake" (Matt. 5:11).

How could we possibly consider such suffering to be a blessing?

Only by faith that knows and believes Jesus, the same faith found in the saints of old listed in Hebrews 11, the same faith at work in the Oxford Martyrs, the same faith expressed by believers throughout the world in our day as they are persecuted for the name of Christ, the same faith exhibited by Peter (Acts 5:40–42) and commended to us.

Likely, for most of us there has been little risk in speaking up for the Christian faith. But that seems to be changing. While tepid cultural Christianity may be welcomed or at least tolerated because it has no biblical backbone, the Christianity Peter champions that exalts Jesus Christ and defends the truth greatly threatens cultural compromise and is under serious attack.

Peter urges us not to be afraid of their threats nor even to be troubled, but instead to look to our Lord Jesus and recognize His reign on high for the sake of His church and His presence with us for witness (Matt. 28:18–20). For our part, we must "always be ready to give a defense to everyone who asks you a reason for the hope that is in you, with meekness and fear" (1 Peter 3:15). In other words, when people open the door for us to explain ourselves as to why we believe as we do, we want to be prepared. Our preparation involves two things: a willingness and eagerness for the opportunity, and a reasoned account that explains what God has done in the person and work of His Son for our salvation.

PRINCIPLE

Every believer is a witness.
How would you explain the hope that is yours in Christ?

Chapter 32

Winsome Witness

"...give a defense to everyone who asks you a reason for the hope
that is in you, with meekness and fear;
having a good conscience..."
(1 Peter 3:15–16)

Have you ever heard the expression "Bible bashing"? It can be done from the pulpit or in person by aggressively using the Bible to twist arms and force submission. I remember sitting in on an evangelistic visit being done as part of an evangelism training event. The trainer was engaged in a full court press by rolling out a rehearsed presentation of the gospel, in relentless pursuit of the captive audience until he submitted. It was clear to me that the resulting profession was not to Christ but to get away from the relentless pressure. I returned on my own the next day to talk about it with the person, and it became clear to me that he had no clue what he had signed up for.

Peter speaks against the practice of strong-arming. Even though he believes that the Bible is the inspired Word of God Himself and that it holds the message of life, he does not instruct us to cram it down anyone's throat but instead to appeal to such a person. We are to reason together, giving a defense for the hope that is ours in Christ and explaining that he or she, too, can have that sure hope through faith in Him. The picture Peter paints is one of dialog not domination. He says we are to engage others with meekness and fear, which can be otherwise expressed as gentleness and respect. We are not to talk *at* people, but *with* them, regarding them as the image bearers of God that they are, and engaging them in the logical flow of creation, rebellion, alienation, reconciliation, and redemption laid out in God's holy Word.

An approach of gentleness and respect leaves room for the

Spirit whose role alone it is to convince, convict, and convert. In his second letter to Timothy, Paul emphasizes that the Bible is the very Word of the living God, able to make a person wise for salvation through faith in Jesus (2 Tim. 3:15–17). Yet Paul's charge to Timothy is to bring that Word to bear, not as a sledgehammer, but with patience and instruction as he engages others for teaching, reproof, correction, and training in righteousness (2 Tim. 4:2).

If we would speak the truth in love, we must do so with these four qualities: gentleness, respect, patience, and instruction, knowing that it is the Holy Spirit who makes alive and gives ears to hear and hearts to receive and wills to embrace Jesus Christ as He is offered in the gospel. We must see our roles as spiritual midwives, not as spiritual salesmen. The offense we give must be that of the gospel that is the stench of death to those who are perishing but the aroma of life to those God has granted life (see 2 Cor. 2:15–17).

Handling ourselves and our message winsomely does not mean that we will not be reviled. But then conflict avoidance is not our goal, just as our goal is not to sell a product. Our goal is to communicate Christ with a clear conscience so that "when they defame you as evildoers, those who revile your good conduct in Christ may be ashamed. For it is better, if it is the will of God, to suffer for doing good than for doing evil" (1 Peter 3:16–17).

PRINCIPLE

In our relating the gospel, Christ makes His appeal through us. What is the difference between a spiritual midwife and a spiritual salesman?

Chapter 33

It's All About Jesus

"For Christ also suffered once for sins, the just for the unjust, that
He might bring us to God, being put to death in the flesh but
made alive by the Spirit. . ."
(1 Peter 3:18)

Peter begins his letter by identifying himself as an apostle of Jesus Christ. His first words in the body of his letter have to do with God's mercy in Christ and the living hope that is found in the resurrection of Jesus Christ from the dead. He will close his epistle with the benediction: "Peace to you all who are in Christ Jesus." Jesus is the subject and focal point, touching every teaching, every perspective, every command. Like one of those block puzzles, if we were to remove Jesus, the whole thing would fall apart.

So it is no surprise that Peter, in addressing our conduct as aliens and sojourners, brings to bear the saving, substitutionary, sacrificial work of Jesus Christ as the beating heart animating our lives as His disciples. This gospel of grace through faith in Christ is not novel to the New Testament; it anticipated and prefigured from Genesis on. As Peter has pointed out, the descriptions of God's old covenant people apply to new covenant believers as well (1 Peter 2:4–10), one people in Christ. Peter points us to Christ in three ways.

Jesus is God's only provision for salvation. "Christ also suffered once for sins, the just for the unjust, that He might bring us to God, being put to death in the flesh but made alive by the Spirit" (1 Peter 3:18). Jesus is the Christ of God, sent from His side to stand in our place, suffer the punishment we deserve, and gain a victory we could not. He bestows not merely a gift from God but God Himself and a restored relationship with Him.

Jesus is the Savior signified throughout Scripture. Peter points us to a familiar account in Genesis. "He went and preached to the spirits in prison, who formerly were disobedient, when once the Divine long-suffering waited in the days of Noah, while the ark was being prepared, in which a few, that is, eight souls, were saved through water" (1 Peter 3:19–20). There was not a different way of salvation in the Old Testament. Rather, portraits of salvation are previews of God's work in Christ, and the preaching of the gospel always speaks to what God will do through His Messiah. The flood of Noah's day that brought destruction to a sinful humanity lifted to safety those placed in the ark by God. That ark pointed to Christ as God's only provision from the wrath to come.

Salvation is received through faith in Christ alone. Saints in the old covenant period were saved by grace through faith in God's Messiah to come. Saints in the new covenant period are saved by grace through faith in God's Messiah who has come. Baptism is a sign of covenant initiation that points to God's promise of salvation in that Messiah, a salvation that is received by grace through faith. Peter emphasizes that water baptism does not save (3:21), but it points to the Christ who does cleanse from sin (3:22). That's why at Pentecost Peter called for baptism in becoming part of the visible church (Acts 2:38) when he applied to them God's covenant promise first made to Abraham: "For the promise is to you and to your children, and to all who are afar off, as many as the Lord our God will call" (Acts 2:39).

PRINCIPLE

Christ is the heart of the gospel prefigured,
procured, and proclaimed.
Where do you see Jesus when you read the Old Testament?

Chapter 34

Ceasing From Sin

*"Therefore, since Christ suffered for us in the flesh, arm yourselves
also with the same mind. . ."*
(1 Peter 4:1)

Chapter four of 1 Peter begins with a "therefore." Peter is draw-
ing a conclusion and driving it home to us for the conduct of
our Christian walk. He writes: "Therefore, since Christ suffered for
us in the flesh, arm yourselves also with the same mind, for he who
has suffered in the flesh has ceased from sin" (1 Peter 4:1). What is
Peter driving home to us? In what way have we ceased from sin? If
we are honest with ourselves, sin seems very much alive in us. We
find ourselves prone to wander, prone to leave the God we love. We
readily identify with Paul in Romans 7 when he describes his battle
with indwelling sin and declares himself "wretched."

The "therefore" that begins the section points us to how we have
ceased from sin. Peter has just spoken of baptism saving us (3:21)—
not that we are saved by the sacrament of baptism but we are saved
by that which baptism represents, namely, union with Jesus Christ
in His saving work. That's why Peter goes on to talk about Christ's
resurrection and intercession on high for us (3:21–22). Through
fellowship in Christ's sufferings on our behalf, we have a new relationship with sin. While we were in bondage to it, we are now freed
from its power. As Paul explained in Romans 6: "But now having
been set free from sin, and having become slaves of God, you have
your fruit to holiness, and the end, everlasting life" (Rom. 6:22).

When Peter talks about Jesus suffering in the flesh, he is not
simply referring to physical suffering or even psychological suffering. Rather, he is speaking about what theologians call the humiliation of Christ in which the eternal Son of God veiled in human
flesh the glory He had with the Father from all eternity. He took on

true and full humanity, becoming in every way like us except for sin. He suffered the miseries of this life and the cruel death of the cross, and He gained the victory for us. He delivered us from the bondage of sin and dominion of death to no longer live for sin but for God.

Jesus is the Suffering Servant of Isaiah 53. He is the one of whom Peter wrote earlier in his letter, "who Himself bore our sins in His own body on the tree" and so we, having died to sins, might live for righteousness" (1 Peter 2:24). We who died in Christ are to die to sin.

This means that our coming to faith in Christ brings us to a crossroad, a then and now, a before and after. We who were dead in sin are now to live dead to sin and alive in Christ. Peter highlights this kingdom transition when he says that the one in Christ "no longer should live the rest of his time in the flesh for the lusts of men, but for the will of God" (1 Peter 4:2).

Peter is helping us to understand what it means to seek first the kingdom of God and His righteousness, as Jesus expounded in the Sermon on the Mount. Coming under the rule of Christ marks a watershed moment in our lives. Peter emphatically says, "For we have spent enough of our past lifetime in doing the will of the Gentiles—when we walked in lewdness, lusts, drunkenness, revelries, drinking parties, and abominable idolatries" (1 Peter 4:3). When temptation strikes, we are to say, "Enough is enough!"

PRINCIPLE

Devotion to Christ displaces devotion to all else and others.
How does your devotion to Christ show up in the various roles
and responsibilities of your life?

Chapter 35

Preaching to the Dead

*"For this reason the gospel was preached also to those
who are dead. . ."*
(1 Peter 4:6)

Peter has reminded us that we have spent enough time doing what the Gentiles do, and then goes on to lay out a laundry list of sin: lewdness, lusts, drunkenness, revelries, drinking parties, and abominable idolatries. Why does Peter refer to Gentiles? Is he making some sort of point in reference to ethnicity?

Peter is expressing himself the same way Paul did in his letter to the church at Ephesus (Eph. 4:17–19). There Paul described Gentiles as ones dead in sin and separated from the life of God, and so walking in darkness. It's clear that both apostles are speaking about unbelievers when they refer to Gentiles. In Christ, there is one people of God, a people of faith. That includes believing Jews and believing Gentiles. Together, we are a people of the gospel, and the gospel is the gospel of the kingdom ruled by Jesus Christ, to whom all authority in heaven and on earth has been given by virtue of His victory over sin, death, and the grave.

Our new identity and life in Christ mandates a new orientation under the lordship of Christ. Paul sums it up as *putting off* our former manner of life and *putting on* a manner of life that reflects our new status and state of being where we grow in knowledge, righteousness, and holiness. Peter emphasizes the suffering we can expect from being in a world that has no time for Christ. He says that "they think it strange that you do not run with them in the same flood of dissipation, speaking evil of you" (1 Peter 4:4). Peter, however, reminds us that "they will give an account to Him who is ready to judge the living and the dead" (1 Peter 4:5).

The gospel provides for us the only refuge from being judged and declared guilty before God. The writer of Hebrews says that we all face judgment upon our death (Heb. 9:27). But if we rest in the work of Christ by faith, our judgment *precedes* our death, as our Lord Jesus explained: "Most assuredly, I say to you, he who hears My word and believes in Him who sent Me has everlasting life, and shall not come into judgment, but has passed from death into life" (John 5:24).

It is while we are alive, in the flesh of our mortal bodies, that we have opportunity to turn to Christ and escape the judgment to come. That's what Peter is stressing when he says, "For this reason the gospel was preached also to those who are dead, that they might be judged according to men in the flesh, but live according to God in the spirit" (1 Peter 4:6).

Peter is not here speaking of preaching to those who are spiritually dead, although that is the case for all gospel proclamation (Eph. 2:1–10). Nor is he suggesting that those who died have another opportunity to turn to Christ. Rather, he is referring to those who embraced the gospel proclaimed when they were alive but who have since died and are now enjoying the life of Christ while awaiting His return.

The fact that we have already been judged and declared not guilty because of Him who was found guilty in our place in no way promotes sin and license. On the contrary, as ones alive in Christ, we are of those who "no longer should live the rest of his time in the flesh for the lusts of men, but for the will of God" (1 Peter 4:2).

PRINCIPLE

The gospel that brings salvation begets sanctification.
What impact does the grace of God have on your everyday life?

Chapter 36

Love One Another Earnestly

". . .above all things have fervent love for one another. . ."
(1 Peter 4:8)

I wonder what the mood was in Jesus' time with His disciples in the upper room on the night He was betrayed. It must have been joyous in that they were celebrating the Passover as an intimate group that had been together over three years. It was also likely confusing with Jesus washing His disciples' feet, perhaps even a bit comical when Peter went overboard with his protest at Jesus washing his feet. It must have turned somber when Jesus spoke of His betrayal, departure, and death.

Prominent in that time with His disciples, however, was Jesus' discourse. That discourse was sweeping in its purview and permeated with love. At least fifteen times in John 13–17, the term "love" is mentioned. Love is the distinguishing mark of a Christian. This mark is not mere sentimentality; it is expressed in devotion and obedience. That sort of love is exercised in relationship with Jesus. Even more profound, this love establishes us in the mix of the love between the Father and the Son. That's the note on which Jesus closes His discourse when He prays to the Father: "And I have declared to them Your name, and will declare it, that the love with which You loved Me may be in them, and I in them" (John 17:26).

That lesson on love stuck with Peter. It's a topic found throughout his letter. Peter begins to wind down his message by speaking of the "end of all things" (4:7) being at hand, for which he urges them to "be serious and watchful in [their] prayers" (4:7). A few verses later, Peter will refer to the fiery trial to come and pending judgment. But in between, Peter emphasizes love as a matter of supreme importance: "And above all things have fervent love for one another, for 'love will cover a multitude of sins'" (1 Peter

4:8). It may well be that Peter could still hear Jesus' voice in the upper room. "A new commandment I give to you, that you love one another; as I have loved you, that you also love one another. By this all will know that you are My disciples, if you have love for one another" (John 13:34–35).

Peter is writing to disciples of Jesus then and now, the "beloved" (4:12) of the Lord whom Jesus said He was praying for (John 17:20), and he is reissuing Christ's call to love. Love for one another who share a common faith speaks volumes to an unbelieving world. Our model for love is our Lord Himself. What does this love look like? Jesus demonstrated it when He laid aside His garments and took up a towel to wash His disciples' feet. By way of explanation, Jesus said: "This is My commandment, that you love one another as I have loved you. Greater love has no one than this, than to lay down one's life for his friends" (John 15:12–13). Service, sacrifice—these are the driving forces behind Christian love.

The love required of us is seen in forgiving those who sin against us (see Col. 3:12–14). It's seen in showing hospitality, not begrudgingly but willingly (1 Peter 4:9). That's how Christ loved us. That is how Peter will tell shepherds of the church to love the flock (1 Peter 5:2). If we love Jesus, we will love His sheep and serve one another.

PRINCIPLE

The curriculum for Christianity from grade school through graduate studies has to do with love learned from our Savior. What impact does love have on life?

Chapter 37

Serve One Another Faithfully

"As each one has received a gift, minister it to one another. . ."
(1 Peter 4:10)

Two fours and two twelves. Those are chapter numbers in the New Testament epistles that focus on spiritual gifts. Romans 12 and 1 Corinthians 12 each lends perspective to the use of spiritual gifts as well as to their variety. Ephesians 4 and 1 Peter 4 address spiritual gifts more broadly. All the passages, however, have one thing in common. Gifts are given by God not for the aggrandizement of self but for the good of the body.

Peter puts it this way: "As each one has received a gift, minister it to one another, as good stewards of the manifold grace of God" (1 Peter 4:10). "Each" speaks to us as individuals. No one in the body of Christ is without some sort of endowment given by God. Sometimes those gifts will be apparent, such as having ability to sing or play an instrument. Other times, our gifts may come to the fore in the way God blesses others through them, as we go about our ordinary involvement. He also blesses us in that He gives us a special delight and fulfillment in their use, as we see God at work through us.

When we take stock of our talents that God particularly uses, we want to remember that we have received that ability from God (see 1 Cor. 4:7). There is no room for pride. As such, we are stewards of that gift and entrusted with the responsibility for its use to God's glory and the good of others. A steward is one who manages something that belongs to someone else. We want to be dedicated, diligent managers of our gifts. Gifts come to us by the Holy Spirit as manifestations of the manifold grace of God.

Throughout the body of believers we see diverse abilities and talents. Peter emphasizes that we not only serve God in the exercise of our gifts; we serve one another. Together, we are greater than our individual parts, not in competition with one another but in completion of one another. It is helpful to think of our gifts as part of a jigsaw puzzle. Each of us is unique and fits in somewhere in God's design for the whole. It would be derelict of us to disengage ourselves from God's design.

Peter identifies two categories of gifts: speaking and serving. "If anyone speaks, let him speak as the oracles of God. If anyone ministers, let him do it as with the ability which God supplies" (1 Peter 4:11). In other words, there are those gifted in teaching, knowing the Word of God and being able to communicate it, and those gifted in serving, ministering through their practical efforts. We might see elders and deacons as the ordained roles representative of these categories (see Phil. 1:1).

Whatever we do, however, we are to exercise our gifts for the glory of God. Peter goes on: ". . . that in all things God may be glorified through Jesus Christ, to whom belong the glory and the dominion forever and ever. Amen" (1 Peter 4:11). Our gifts are not for personal gain or glory but for the blessing of others and for the building up of the body, to the glory of God.

PRINCIPLE

Spiritual gifts are to foster unity through diversity.
How does God use you in service to others?

Chapter 38

Trials and Triumph

". . .rejoice to the extent that you partake of Christ's sufferings. . ."
(1 Peter 4:13)

Even though we might see it coming, even though we are given a heads up to expect it, we can still be surprised by suffering. In the upper room with Peter and the other disciples, on the verge of securing victory through His death and resurrection, Jesus brought His discourse to a close with these words: "These things I have spoken to you, that in Me you may have peace. In the world you will have tribulation; but be of good cheer, I have overcome the world" (John 16:33).

We are told to expect tribulation. It is a given while we are in this world. In alerting us to it, Jesus injected words of hope and encouragement when He spoke of His overcoming the world. That does not mean, however, that our trials and tribulations are not painful or a challenge to handle.

It is against the background of our Lord's statement that Peter addresses us. He captures our attention by addressing us as "beloved." We are ones loved by Jesus. We meet suffering not as ones abandoned or neglected or abused but as ones deeply, unwaveringly loved. With that salutation, Peter nestles us in the arms of our Lord Jesus as we undergo fiery trials.

Peter issues a caution and a calling. "Beloved, do not think it strange concerning the fiery trial which is to try you, as though some strange thing happened to you; but rejoice to the extent that you partake of Christ's sufferings, that when His glory is revealed, you may also be glad with exceeding joy" (1 Peter 4:12–13).

Peter is reminding us that Christ's road to glory was fraught with suffering, and we who bear His name walk that same path. Our Lord taught this as well: "If the world hates you, you know that it hated Me before it hated you. If you were of the world, the world would love its own. Yet because you are not of the world, but I chose you out of the world, therefore the world hates you. If they persecuted Me, they will also persecute you" (John 15:18–20).

What does it mean for us to "partake of Christ's sufferings" (v. 13)? Paul put it even more surprisingly: "I now rejoice in my sufferings for you, and fill up in my flesh what is lacking in the afflictions of Christ, for the sake of His body, which is the church" (Col. 1:24). Paul was not suggesting that Jesus' suffering was inadequate. Rather, he meant that there is ongoing suffering as the Spirit applies Christ's work in the building of His church. We who know and serve Jesus share in His sufferings while we sojourn in this fallen world "that when His glory is revealed, you may also be glad with exceeding joy" (1 Peter 4:13).

Are you insulted for Christ? Are you reviled for your witness? Have you suffered loss for the sake of Christ? Know this by faith: you are blessed. Why? How? Because "the Spirit of glory and of God rests upon you" (1 Peter 4:14), and that Spirit unites you to Him who overcame for you.

PRINCIPLE

The road to glory is pitted with the potholes of suffering.
In what way have you suffered loss for the sake of Christ?

Chapter 39

Suffering as a Christian

*"Yet if anyone suffers as a Christian, let him not be ashamed, but
let him glorify God in this matter."*
(1 Peter 4:16)

We find in our English translation the word "but" four times
in 1 Peter 4:13–16. Three different Greek words, however,
are represented. Verse 13 holds a strong adversative (*alla*). In stark
distinction at being shocked and dismayed by suffering we are to
be expectant of it and even to delight ourselves in it. Rather than
resisting suffering or resigning ourselves to it, we are to rejoice in
it as something inherent to fellowship in the sufferings endured by
our Lord Jesus (Acts 5:41).

In verse 16, the word translated "but" (*de*) serves to further the
flow of thought, setting up a mild contrast. "Yet if anyone suffers
as a Christian, let him not be ashamed, but let him glorify God in
this matter" (1 Peter 4:16). Shame to self is contrasted with glory
to God. We are not to shrink back at experiencing disgrace and
scorn and abuse at the hands of an unbelieving world. Rather, we
are stand up and press on under it to the glory of God, in the model
of our Lord Jesus.

The third word Peter uses to press home his point carries yet
another emphasis. "But let none of you suffer as a murderer, a thief,
an evildoer, or as a busybody in other people's matters" (1 Peter
4:15). Here Peter is driving home a logical inference, setting up
a contrast of character. The word translated "but" (*gar*) conveys a
sense of cause or explanation.

This section of 1 Peter with its contrariness reminds us of something important that belongs to the Christian life. Though we were
at home in darkness, now it is alien to us. The trajectory of our
lives is radically different. We now have a hope and home in eternal

glory. As to our conduct, Peter has told us: "... as obedient children, not conforming yourselves to the former lusts, as in your ignorance; but as He who called you is holy, you also be holy in all your conduct" (1 Peter 1:14–15). Much of Peter's epistle has contrasted this before and after, and directed us in what it means and what it looks like to bear the name of Jesus before an unbelieving world.

We will suffer in this world but when we do, we must suffer "as a Christian" (v. 16; compare v. 14). This is one of only three times in the New Testament where the designation "Christian" is used and the only one outside the book of Acts. To be called a Christian is to be identified with our Lord Jesus Christ. We follow His teachings. We rest in His promises. We share in His sufferings now and we share in the glory to come. Like Him, we suffer for righteousness' sake, not as "a murderer, a thief, an evildoer" (v. 15).

Peter drives home his message about suffering as a Christian by speaking of judgment. "For the time has come for judgment to begin at the house of God; and if it begins with us first, what will be the end of those who do not obey the gospel of God?" (1 Peter 4:17). God is at work sanctifying those He loves. Trials and adversities are kilns through which we die to self, and Christ is formed in us. But we will not endure the eternal judgment as will those who reject "the Christ, the Son of the living God" (Matt. 16:16).

PRINCIPLE

The name "Christian" gives us identity and governs our activity.
How is being a Christian different from any other way
you might describe yourself?

Chapter 40

Trust and Obey

". . .commit their souls to God in doing good. . ."
(1 Peter 4:19)

One of the most well-known concluding statements in Scripture is found in the Old Testament book of Ecclesiastes. "Let us hear the conclusion of the whole matter: fear God and keep His commandments, for this is man's all" (Eccles. 12:13). Not only is this the summation of the book; it encompasses humanity's overall purpose. That statement serves as a corrective lens to life for safe passage in our journey through a fallen world, lest we draw wrong inferences based on our experience. When we behold the righteous faltering and the wicked prospering, when we witness seeming chaos and contradiction, we may draw mistaken opinions about God and His dealings with us. Only through the fear of God that knows God lives and reigns will we find our bearings, rather than trying to find them "under the sun" with a sin-warped world as our point of reference.

In the same way, Peter issues a twofold conclusion that seems to carry the weight of his entire letter and set the tone for the conduct of our lives. "Therefore let those who suffer according to the will of God commit their souls to Him in doing good, as to a faithful Creator" (1 Peter 4:19).

Just as Peter has spoken of accountability to God (4:17–18), so does Ecclesiastes: "For God will bring every work into judgment, including every secret thing, whether good or evil" (Eccles. 12:14). Our lives are lived in relationship to and relationship with our God and Father. Ecclesiastes calls us to exercise faith by fearing God and keeping His commandments. Peter also calls us to commit ourselves to our Creator who is faithful to Himself and to His Word, and to live in obedience to Him. Peter opened his letter by saying that we were chosen for obedience (1:2, 14; see also Eph. 2:10; Titus 2:11–14), and he reiterates that here. Throughout his letter, Peter has described to us the character of God, His work of redemption, and the reality of our suffering. Now he calls us to the exercise of faith by committing ourselves to God and doing what is right. We lean in to the storms of life and press on in our earthly calling toward our heavenly hope in Christ, walking as He walked.

The key phrase that Peter wants us to latch on to as we embark on a journey of trusting and obeying is suffering "according to the will of God" (v. 19). Through that perspective, we submit ourselves to God's providence in our lives that governs all that comes to pass, trusting that He does all things well, and we commit ourselves to a life of compliance with His revealed will (see Deut. 29:29). These two aspects dovetail in the suffering of our Lord Jesus, "who for the joy that was set before Him endured the cross, despising the shame, and has sat down at the right hand of the throne of God" (Heb. 12:2).

PRINCIPLE

A life of faith fears God and follows His will.
What does it mean to trust God at all times
and obey Him in all things?

Chapter 41

Shepherds and Saints

"Shepherd the flock of God which is among you. . ."
(1 Peter 5:2)

"I don't need to be part of a local church." Perhaps that's something you've heard a fellow believer say, or have even said yourself. People reject membership in a congregation for a variety of reasons. I know some who have been deeply hurt by their pastor and not only left that church but steered clear of any church to avoid a similar experience. Some will defiantly insist that the membership that counts is with the invisible church, the spiritual elect of God, and that being counted on a membership roll of a visible church of professing believers counts for nothing. But whatever led to that conclusion, it is contrary to the design of our Lord Jesus for the protection, maturity, and mobilization of His disciples.

Peter has just spoken of spiritual gifts and the importance of using them for the blessing of others. Other passages that address spiritual gifts make it clear that the primary outlet for their exercise is the local congregation (1 Cor. 12; Eph. 4:11–16). The church also becomes visible by its structure. The writer of Hebrews speaks of a people accountable to its leaders (Heb. 13:17) and leaders responsible for those under their care (Heb. 13:7). Converts throughout the book of Acts were enfolded into communities under the care of elders.

Peter identifies himself as an elder and addresses fellow elders who have the responsibility for the flock under their care. He urges elders to "shepherd the flock of God which is among you, serving as overseers" (1 Peter 5:2). The term "elder" refers to the spiritual maturity of a candidate. He is not to be a new convert but one seasoned in the faith. The qualifications laid out in 1 Timothy 3 and Titus 1 lean heavy on the character of the man. The word "pastor" means "shepherd" and involves overseeing the flock for their sanctification and service for the work of the kingdom. An elder's role is that of shepherding the flock according to the model of the chief Shepherd (John 10; Heb. 13:20–21). He carries out that responsibility in three ways: by prayer, by ministry of the Word, and by personal example.

Peter stresses that elders are to exercise their charge not for self glory or personal gain but as servant leaders of those in their care. They are to act "not by compulsion but willingly, not for dishonest gain but eagerly; nor as being lords over those entrusted to [them], but being examples to the flock" (1 Peter 5:2–3).

What this means is that those set apart as elders must be constantly on guard against pride and arrogance, lest they misuse their office and abuse the flock. When Paul meets with the elders of the Ephesian church, he calls them to faithful exercise of their calling but he begins by having them look first to themselves. "Therefore take heed to yourselves and to all the flock, among which the Holy Spirit has made you overseers, to shepherd the church of God which He purchased with His own blood" (Acts 20:28). There is not a double standard for shepherds and sheep. Both are under the same Lord. Only in that way can elders be effective examples so that the sheep can follow them as they follow Christ.

Elders are not to exercise oversight for personal gain but that does not mean there is not gain to be had. "When the Chief Shepherd appears, you will receive the crown of glory that does not fade away" (1 Peter 5:4).

PRINCIPLE

Elders learn about shepherding by looking to the chief Shepherd.
Why is involvement with a local church so important?

Chapter 42

Danger of Pride

"God resists the proud,
But gives grace to the humble."
(1 Peter 5:5)

J esus came not to be served but to serve and to give His life a ransom for many. That is the model for Christ's shepherds. False shepherds think only of themselves and how they can use the sheep for their own gain (Ezek. 34:1–4). Peter would have heard Jesus taking the Pharisees to task for such self-serving "ministry." True shepherds, on the other hand, follow the model of the Good Shepherd (John 10:11–28). They sacrifice themselves to know the sheep, feed them, pursue the wandering, rescue the ensnared, tend to the infirm, and equip them to do the Father's will.

The hallmark of the shepherd after Christ's heart is humility. Pride produces the fruit of domineering and craving for selfish gain. Humility operates in the fear of the Lord, saying, "Not unto me, not unto me, but to God alone be the glory." Humility recognizes that station, calling, aptitude, and opportunity come from God and are to be consecrated to Him (cf. 1 Peter 4:8–11). Humility establishes itself in the hand of God for the work to be done, knowing full well that it is only by Him that the shepherd's ministry will be effective.

This hallmark of humility, however, is required not only of leaders but of every disciple of Jesus Christ. Peter drives this home when he says: "Likewise you younger people, submit yourselves to your elders. Yes, all of you be submissive to one another, and be clothed with humility, for 'God resists the proud, but gives grace to the humble'" (1 Peter 5:5). Being part of Christian community, the local church, calls for us to lay aside independence of pride and autonomy of self-rule and instead exercise humility toward those who have spiritual oversight over us and to one another. Those who refuse local church alignment display hubris rather than humility and put themselves in the position of opposing God and depriving themselves of the means of grace found in the local body.

There is another aspect to consider. Peter uses the statement that "God resists the proud, but gives grace to the humble" (v. 5) as a hinge. It looks back to the need for us to be submissive to God's design, to those He places over us, and to one another. It also looks ahead to spiritual danger we face through our enemy the devil, an adversary in adversity. Humility will keep us from wandering from the sheep pen, making ourselves easy prey for Satan. The writer of Hebrews draws our attention to the importance of involvement in Christian community, both for encouragement (Heb. 10:23–25) and also for protection from enticements of the evil one. "Beware, brethren, lest there be in any of you an evil heart of unbelief in departing from the living God; but exhort one another daily, while it is called 'Today,' lest any of you be hardened through the deceitfulness of sin" (Heb. 3:12–13).

Every aspect of our lives as Christians is contingent on God and dependent upon Him. We can do all things through Him who strengthens us (Phil. 4:16). We work out our salvation with fear and trembling only because God is at work in us both to will and do for His good pleasure (Phil. 4:12–13). Unless we abide in Christ as the vine, we will not bear fruit; but by abiding in Him, we will bear fruit—fruit that is genuine, abundant, and that will last (John 15:4–5). Only through humility will we rest in Christ and find grace necessary for growth.

PRINCIPLE

Pride is the wellspring of idolatry.
Why does God resist the proud?

Chapter 43

Our Adversary the Devil

"Be sober, be vigilant. . ."
(1 Peter 5:8)

On the eve of His crucifixion, Jesus took Peter, James, and John to the Garden of Gethsemane where He poured out His heart in prayer, committing Himself to the will of His Father for the mission of redemption. Three times Jesus returned to His waiting disciples; and three times He found them sleeping. He roused them with words of warning: "Watch and pray, lest you enter into temptation. The spirit indeed is willing, but the flesh is weak" (Matt. 26:41).

No doubt Peter had that admonition in mind when he wrote to believers: "Be sober, be vigilant; because your adversary the devil walks about like a roaring lion, seeking whom he may devour" (1 Peter 5:8). Just as we would be alert and on guard for an assailant intent on our harm, we must have our wits about us and be wide awake in view of an ever-present danger for us in this fallen world (Gal. 1:3–5).

Peter describes the devil as a roaring lion on the prowl, intent on devouring us. How do we see Satan on the prowl around us? How does he look to devour us? In John 12:31 Jesus described the devil as "the ruler of this world," meaning that in this fallen world we sojourn in his kingdom of darkness, death, and destruction. We can expect the institutions of this world to be instruments of Satan, advocating what is often contrary to the will of God yet couched in noble terms. We see this happening today in secular educational institutions, "righteous" political ideologies, and churches that have become unmoored from the Bible, what Jesus describes as "synagogues of Satan" (Rev. 3:8–9).

Paul speaks of "wicked and evil men" (2 Thess. 3:2) who oppose him, yet in parallel he says: "But the Lord is faithful, who will establish you and guard you from the evil one" (2 Thess. 3:2–3). The apostle is even more direct in his word to the church at Corinth: "For such are false apostles, deceitful workers, transforming themselves into apostles of Christ. And no wonder! For Satan himself transforms himself into an angel of light. Therefore it is no great thing if his ministers also transform themselves into ministers of righteousness, whose end will be according to their works" (2 Cor. 11:13–15). We confront the evil one not only through his schemes but also through his agents. Peter himself was charged by Jesus as an instrument of the evil one when he sought to thwart the will of God (Matt. 16:21–23).

Peter instructs us to *resist* the efforts of our enemy the devil (v. 9), who seeks to devour us. The word translated "resist" means "to stand against," the very same tactic advocated by Paul to the Ephesians (Eph. 6:10–14). We are to stand firm in Christ's deliverance against the devil's accusations, stand firm in Christ's word against the devil's deceptions, and stand firm in Christ's power against the devil's temptations. Only in Christ do we overcome and have peace in this present, evil age (1 Peter 5:14).

Jesus alerted Peter to the intentions of the devil. "Simon, Simon! Indeed, Satan has asked for you, that he may sift you as wheat. But I have prayed for you, that your faith should not fail; and when you have returned to Me, strengthen your brethren" (Luke 22:31–32). By informing us that the devil is on the prowl for our harm and by calling us to stand firm in the faith, Peter is carrying out Christ's charge to strengthen us for spiritual opposition in our sojourning.

PRINCIPLE

We resist the devil by resting in Christ.
How do we go about resting in Him?

Chapter 44

Anguish Given Way to Glory

". . .the God of all grace, who called us to His eternal glory. . ."
(1 Peter 5:10)

Peter has told us to expect suffering in this life for the sake of Christ, how to suffer appropriate to our calling in Christ, and something of the joy of suffering now in light of the glory to come. His entire letter has pastorally ministered to us in the suffering inherent in our sojourning, equipping us to live for the sake of Christ in what can be an inhospitable world. As he winds up his epistle, Peter closes with an embrace of perspective and hope. "But may the God of all grace, who called us to His eternal glory by Christ Jesus, after you have suffered a while, perfect, establish, strengthen, and settle you" (1 Peter 5:10).

When the Thessalonian Christians were confused and grieving, Paul reminded them that their hope was not wishful thinking, but an assured reality that rested in God's purpose in election secured by His Son (1 Thess. 5:9). That future hope colors present life (1 Thess. 5:4–5). Because their hope was secure and sure, they need not grieve as those who had no hope (1 Thess. 4:13–14). Amidst their tears, they could find comfort, encouragement, and courage in Christ. Peter has taken the same approach in his letter, addressing us as a people of hope given by God, grounded in Christ, and growing toward glory.

Peter again describes our suffering as but for "a while" (5:10; see 1:6). Our suffering may seem interminable but it is fleeting in view of eternity. It will be swallowed up in the glory that is ours in Christ. Even now, that glory exerts a gravitational pull, lightening the cares that weigh us down. Earlier Peter said: "Therefore humble yourselves under the mighty hand of God, that He may exalt you in due time, casting all your care upon Him, for He cares for you"

(1 Peter 5:6–7). Our God and Father gives us strength to bear up under our burdens and will one day relieve us of them entirely, all because Jesus bore our shame and sorrows.

Peter expresses our hope this way: "But may the God of all grace, who called us to His eternal glory by Christ Jesus, after you have suffered a while, perfect, establish, strengthen, and settle you" (1 Peter 5:10). Our future is in the hands of our God, as is our present. He is the God of all grace, who lavishes good gifts upon us and bestows upon us every blessing through Jesus Christ. Paul turns up the volume in expressing our hope: "Now may the God of hope fill you with all joy and peace in believing, that you may abound in hope by the power of the Holy Spirit" (Rom. 15:13).

To drive home the fact that God will complete what He began and that our hope is secure, Peter piles word upon word, each conveying completion. What is started will be finished. What has been promised will be fulfilled. What has been formed will be unshaken. We who have sojourned through many dangers, toils, and snares will be settled in the inheritance with Jesus prepared for us.

It's no wonder that in reflecting on the glory and certainty of these things, Peter erupts in doxology. "To Him be the glory and the dominion forever and ever. Amen" (1 Peter 5:11).

PRINCIPLE

Our sufferings now are not worth comparing to
the glory that awaits us.
How do you allow the storm clouds of trial to obscure the
brilliance of the hope that continues to shine?

Chapter 45

Sealed with a Kiss

"Peace to you all who are in Christ Jesus. Amen."
(1 Peter 5:14)

Peter signs off his epistle by issuing some concluding remarks. His comments are not mere niceties. Rather, they punctuate what he has said in the body of his letter.

He begins: "By Silvanus, our faithful brother as I consider him, I have written to you briefly, exhorting and testifying that this is the true grace of God in which you stand" (1 Peter 5:12). Earlier, Peter spoke of Christian community. Now he mentions a fellow believer by name. It may be that Silvanus was Peter's scribe or he may have carried the letter. Though Peter's letter has been filled with the nourishment of truth for the sustenance of our souls, he regards it as brief. There's much more he could have said, but what he has written is intended to shore up our faith, highlight our hope, and urge us home in the race set before us. It's noteworthy that Peter speaks of the "true" grace of God. That is a reminder that, in this world, we will face counterfeit teaching, and that we need to stand firm in what has come to us as the Word of God, testing the ways and wisdom of the world by it.

Peter continues: "She who is in Babylon, elect together with you, greets you; and so does Mark my son" (1 Peter 5:13). In speaking of the "she" who is "elect together with you," Peter is referring to other believers, those mentioned in his salutation (1:2). Though there are many local communities of Christians throughout the world, there is but one church that shares a common hope and common calling, serving a common Lord on our common journey. This world is not our home. We are pilgrims for Christ in an inhospitable environment, where we experience troubles and tribulations for the cause of Christ and His kingdom. In that sense, we are all in Babylon, a reference to a world in rebellion against God (Gen. 11:1–9; Rev. 18) that will one day be brought to judgment and destroyed (2 Peter 3:10). We might think of ourselves as Daniel who was exiled to Babylon, yet who remained faithful to the true God and served Him in the roles and opportunities given him in that land. All of us as citizens of heaven look forward to a kingdom that will not be destroyed but will endure into eternity.

Peter brings greetings from other believers and from John Mark, his disciple who authored the Gospel account that bears the name Mark. Peter urges them and us to greet one another with a kiss of love. Paul says the same sort of thing in some of his letters. "Greet one another with a holy kiss. The churches of Christ greet you" (Rom. 16:16). We greet one another as a holy people who, by grace, have kissed the Son, God's Messiah (Ps. 2:12). Peter calls it a "kiss of love" (5:14) shared by those loved by God (1:2; 4:12), who love His Son (1:8), and are called to love one another (3:8).

Living as aliens and sojourners in a world where we can expect tribulation and opposition is no easy thing. To us, Peter extends these closing words: "Peace to you all who are in Christ Jesus. Amen" (5:14). Those words are not mere sentiment, like we might bid someone farewell by saying, "Take care." Rather, they are words of truth and grace, grounded in our fellowship in the saving work of Jesus Christ, our living hope.

PRINCIPLE

*God has given us His Word and Spirit and
one another for the journey.
How can you make the most of His provision?*

Epilogue

A Song for the Journey: "For All the Saints"

For all the saints who from their labors rest,
who Thee by faith before the world confessed,
Thy name, O Jesus, be forever blest.
Alleluia! Alleluia!

Thou wast their rock, their fortress, and their might;
Thou, Lord, their captain in the well-fought fight;
Thou, in the darkness drear, their one true light.
Alleluia! Alleluia!

Oh, may Thy soldiers, faithful, true, and bold
fight as the saints who nobly fought of old
and win with them the victor's crown of gold.
Alleluia! Alleluia!

Oh, blest communion, fellowship divine!
We feebly struggle, they in glory shine;
yet all are one in thee, for all are Thine.
Alleluia! Alleluia!

And when the fight is fierce, the warfare long,
steals on the ear the distant triumph song,
and hearts are brave again and arms are strong.
Alleluia! Alleluia!

The golden evening brightens in the west;
soon, soon to faithful warriors cometh rest;
sweet is the calm of paradise the blest.
Alleluia! Alleluia!

But, lo! there breaks a yet more glorious day;
the saints triumphant rise in bright array;
the King of glory passes on His way.
Alleluia! Alleluia!

From earth's wide bounds, from ocean's farthest coast,
through gates of pearl streams in the countless host,
singing to Father, Son, and Holy Ghost,
Alleluia! Alleluia!

William Walsham How (1864, Public Domain)

Companion Volume

This devotional walks readers through the epistle of James, discovering faith as a key theme of this letter. With pastoral insight, Stanley D. Gale helps us understand James's portrayal of a living faith that clings fervently to our Father in heaven and results in following Him faithfully through the trials of this life. Each devotion is followed by two questions aimed at doing the word, whereby readers put into practice what they have learned. This devotional can be used privately, but its brevity makes it well-suited for reading the segment aloud with fellow believers, discussing it together, and supporting each other in prayer and encouragement.

"This devotional commentary is biblical, pastoral, accessible, encouraging, and clear, making it ideal for any individual or small group who wants to put their faith into action."
—Daniel M. Doriani, Covenant Theological Seminary

"With pastoral warmth and practical awareness of the issues God's people face in today's world, Stan shines the light of James's wisdom into our daily experience. Read, reflect, and discover God's encouragement through James."
—Mark G. Johnston, Trinity Church, Richhill, Northern Ireland

"Reading *A Living Faith* is like having your own personal biblical teacher by your side speaking into your spirit words of daily encouragement and inspiration. I know that when I pick up something Stan Gale has written, I'm picking up something biblically solid that I can trust—and you can too."
—Leslie Montgomery, author of *Redemptive Suffering*

"Stan's mastery of Scripture and theology, his keen attention to daily experience, and his winsome pastoral manner make strolling through this book not only a vivid learning experience but a true delight."
—T. M. Moore, The Fellowship of Ailbe

"When you travel through an excellent book such as James, a worthy guide is essential. I have known Stan for many years. I have watched him care for people as their pastor. I have benefited from his careful study of Scripture. He is a fine guide who understands you, and he understands James."
—Edward T. Welch, Christian Counseling and Educational Foundation

A Living Faith: A Devotional Journey through James
Reformation Heritage Books | ISBN 979-8-88686-072-6
Paperback | 112pp

Also by Stanley D. Gale

A Living Faith: A Devotional Journey through James

A Vine-Ripened Life: Spiritual Fruitfulness through Abiding in Christ

Finding Forgiveness: Discovering the Healing Power of the Gospel

Making Sanity Out of Vanity: Christian Realism in the Book of Ecclesiastes

Re: velation: Seeing Jesus. Seeing Self. Standing Firm

The Christian's Creed: Embracing the Apostolic Faith

The Prayer of Jehoshaphat: Seeing Beyond Life's Storms

Warfare Witness: Contending with Spiritual Opposition in Everyday Evangelism

What is Spiritual Warfare? (Basics of the Faith)

Why Do We Pray? (Basics of the Faith)

www.ingramcontent.com/pod-product-compliance
Lightning Source LLC
Chambersburg PA
CBHW070727130626
46553CB00005B/2184